The Weaponizing
of Biology

D1519449

ALSO BY MARC E. VARGO

*The Mossad: Six Landmark Missions
of the Israeli Intelligence Agency,
1960–1990* (McFarland, 2015)

*Women of the Resistance: Eight Who
Defied the Third Reich* (McFarland, 2012)

The Weaponizing of Biology

Bioterrorism, Biocrime and Biohacking

MARC E. VARGO

McFarland & Company, Inc., Publishers

Jefferson, North Carolina

LIBRARY OF CONGRESS CATALOGUING-IN-PUBLICATION DATA

Names: Vargo, Marc E., 1954– author.
Title: The weaponizing of biology : bioterrorism, biocrime and
    biohacking / Marc E. Vargo.
Description: Jefferson, North Carolina : McFarland & Company,
    Inc., Publishers, 2017 | Includes bibliographical references and
    index.
Identifiers: LCCN 2017029080 | ISBN 9781476665429 (softcover :
    alk. paper) ∞
Subjects: LCSH: Bioterrorism—History. | Biological weapons—
    History. | Biological warfare—History.
Classification: LCC HV6433.3 .V37 2017 | DDC 363.325/3—dc23
LC record available at https://lccn.loc.gov/2017029080

BRITISH LIBRARY CATALOGUING DATA ARE AVAILABLE

ISBN (print) 978-1-4766-6542-9
ISBN (ebook) 978-1-4766-2933-9

Front cover images © 2017 iStock

Printed in the United States of America

McFarland & Company, Inc., Publishers
    Box 611, Jefferson, North Carolina 28640
        www.mcfarlandpub.com

For Eric and Adam Vargo

Table of Contents

Introduction

"Evil is only good perverted," writes Henry Wadsworth Longfellow in his narrative poem, *The Golden Legend*.[1] Certainly there is truth in the renowned poet's words, with the corruption of good being readily observable throughout the course of human history, perhaps most notably when that which was intended for the benefit of humankind has been upturned and used as a truncheon against it.

The discipline of biology offers an example, a field of study in which scientists' insights into the intricacies of life have at times been misused by malevolent actors committed to delivering agony and death, and in a most insidious manner: through the spread of disease. And this is not a recent development. Biological aggression in all of its varieties has, for centuries, been a bane to humanity, a practice that cultures around the world have denounced over and again as a singularly despicable and intolerable form of violence. Yet it continues to occur sporadically in both Eastern and Western nations.

In the pages that follow, three categories of biological aggression are examined: bioterrorism, biocrime, and biohacking. Whereas the first two classifications, by definition, culminate in acts of violence, the third category, biohacking, refers to a newly-emergent movement that entails "do-it-yourself biology" (DIYbio) and to date presents only the potential for biological aggression.

The first portion of the book, Part One, examines the fundamental concepts and features of bio-aggression, and, as such, serves as a primer on the subject. The first chapter traces the history of biological warfare from its practice by Chinese warriors nearly five thousand years ago through its use in the Middle Ages and Renaissance to its manifestation in the modern era. In the course of this historical survey, a little-known attempt to deploy a virus to assassinate President Abraham Lincoln in the nineteenth century is revisited, as are pivotal advances in the state-operated biowarfare programs of Germany, Japan, the former Soviet Union, and the United States in the twentieth century. Examined, too, is the growth of non-state bioterrorism in the present century, with a spotlight on the al-Qaeda network.

Chapter 2 centers on the various ideologies that characterize terrorist organizations—political, religious, and special-interest philosophies and agendas—together with such entities' motives, short-term objectives, and long-term goals. Emphasis is placed on the types of extremist groups that biodefense specialists believe are most inclined to use biological weapons, along with the rationales behind the experts' opinions. The discussion concludes by bringing to light a particularly devious form of assault known as a "biocrime," including the ways in which it differs from bioterrorism as well as the reasons that a perpetrator may turn to such an unorthodox mode of aggression.

Biohacking is the subject of Chapter 3, with the text tracing the origin and development of the DIYbio movement, which is currently thriving. It is one in which people from all walks of life, many of whom lack formal training in the life sciences, carry out biological or bioengineering experiments in their homes, community-based workshops, specially designed "hacklabs," or other alternative settings. The potential hazards of this largely amateur endeavor are explored, most notably the concerns voiced by professional microbiologists, geneticists, bioengineers, and biodefense experts. Among their reservations: the possibility that an experiment by a "citizen biologist" may go awry and sicken or kill a swath of the population, or that a group of rogue biohackers may deliberately target individuals or groups with a pathogen, perhaps an augmented, genetically-engineered microbe capable of producing unforeseen damage. The counterarguments of biohacking advocates are presented as well, rejoinders to what they consider their opponents' inflated fears, with such enthusiasts offering several reasons that they believe the benefits of do-it-yourself biology far outweigh the risks of a biological calamity. The discussion concludes with a look at two codes of ethics that biohacking networks have proposed in Europe and North America in an effort to help prevent biological accidents and discourage premeditated pathogenic attacks.

Turning to specific pathogens and toxins, Chapter 4 summarizes the features of those microscopic entities that the Centers for Disease Control and Prevention considers to be prospective agents in a biological offensive. These include the bacteria that produce anthrax, botulism, plague, tularemia, Q fever, and salmonellosis; in addition, the viruses that lead to Ebola and Marburg Virus Diseases, smallpox, and other conditions. The principal modes of pathogen dissemination are also outlined, specifically person-to-person, airborne, foodborne, waterborne, and vector-borne transmission.

Having covered the essentials of biological aggression, the remainder of the book, Part Two, provides an assortment of cases illustrating the diversity of biocrimes and bioterrorism attacks. Chapter 5 revisits several of the former that occurred in the field of medicine in recent years, culminating in a detailed recounting of the notorious case of physician Debora Green and her efforts to use a lethal plant toxin as a weapon. Chapters 6 and 7, on the other hand, showcase the latter, namely two precedent-setting, large-scale bioterrorism attacks orchestrated by extremist religious sects in the United States and Japan. Lastly, Chapter 8 provides an extensive account of the deadly anthrax offensive that followed in the wake of the World Trade Center and Pentagon attacks of September 11, 2001. The text further delves into the possible per-petrators of this historic offensive, including the FBI's third and final suspect whose purported guilt remains debatable to this day.

All in all, the book, by furnishing an up-to-date overview of bioterror-ism, biocrime, and biohacking, serves as a timely reminder of the dangers posed by those individuals and organizations who set out to subvert the life sciences so as to produce illness and death for their own dubious ends. As Longfellow would undoubtedly concur, biological aggression, like chemical and nuclear warfare, is a classic example of "good perverted," as well as a form of violence that carries the potential to endanger the entirety of human-ity itself.

◆ 1 ◆

From Ancient China to al-Qaeda

A Brief History of Biological Warfare

The unleashing of biological agents to produce illness and death is anything but new. Known as "biological warfare" and "germ warfare," individuals and armies alike have long taken part in this notorious practice, not only in foreign lands but in the United States as well. Case in point: the attempted assassination, by biological means, of Abraham Lincoln.

The year was 1864 and the Civil War had been raging for three years. A trauma for the American people, it was also a harrowing ordeal for the commander-in-chief, and not only because of the political burdens it placed on him. In the course of the conflict, Lincoln endured crushing bouts of depression, and, it is today suspected, symptoms of a genetic condition known as spinocerebellar ataxia.[1] He contracted smallpox as well, complaining of dizziness and headache as he prepared to deliver the Gettysburg Address.[2] Shortly thereafter, skin lesions and muscle cramps compounded his misery. Yet despite such maladies, the stalwart leader remained firmly at the helm, choosing, in effect, to place the dispute that was ripping apart the nation before his own health and well-being. A principled decision, it was, of course, one that would render Lincoln physically vulnerable, and this state of affairs would not go unnoticed by his adversaries.

At the opposite end of the moral spectrum, and one such antagonist, was a Kentucky physician by the name of Luke Pryor Blackburn. Described as a "Confederate zealot" by historian Andrew Bell, Blackburn had long abhorred the Lincoln administration and wished to see the president sidelined.[3] For this reason, the doctor, after a three-year stretch during which the commander-in-chief showed no sign of leaving office, decided to take matters into his own hands. Securing the tacit support of Jefferson Davis, head of the Southern "Confederate States of America," Blackburn hatched a plot he

5

believed would remove the commander-in-chief from the political stage once and for all; a plot that would be both diabolical and unprecedented in that it would constitute the first known attempt to transmit a grave illness to a sitting president in order to upend the nation's governance. The doctor knew that another major affliction, such as yellow fever, could bring an end to Lincoln's life.

To launch his nefarious plot, Blackburn sailed to the island of Bermuda, where a yellow fever epidemic was decimating the population. Coming ashore, he was treated to a hearty welcome by the Bermudians, who looked upon him as a godsend because he was an expert in the containment of the disease. Certainly their admiration was warranted. The doctor had previously overseen quarantines to curb outbreaks of yellow fever in New Orleans and the town of Natchez, Mississippi, with his efforts being fruitful and news of his accomplishments spreading far and wide. What the grateful Bermudians did not know, however, is that the outwardly benevolent physician had come to do more than help them control their epidemic; he had also come to help himself to the clothing and bedding of those who had already died in the course of it. An adherent of the fomite theory of yellow fever transmission, Blackburn believed the disease was spread through contact with contaminated materials.

Stuffing eight trunks with the garments and bed linens of deceased yellow fever victims, the doctor shipped the cargo to Nova Scotia, then convinced Godfrey Hyams, a dodgy shoemaker, to transport six of the trunks to the District of Columbia. Hyams was to ensure that the largest of the lot made its way to an auction house in the heart of the capital city, the aim being to inflict the hemorrhagic fever upon Washington's inhabitants, most of all its politicians. "It will kill them at sixty yards," Blackburn boasted.[4] The doctor further directed the courier to leave the remaining pair of trunks in New Bern, North Carolina, and Norfolk, Virginia, two strategically-located towns that Union troops from the North had captured and continued to occupy. Most important, though, the physician handed Hyams a valise thought to be contaminated with yellow fever, inside of which was an assortment of fresh, smart dress shirts. The assumption was that contact with the toxic valise would be sufficient to taint the new garments. "Blackburn instructed Hyams to take the valise, along with a letter, to President Lincoln as a special gift by an anonymous benefactor," writes Edward Steers, Jr. "Blackburn believed that even if Lincoln did not choose to wear the shirts their mere presence would infect him with the deadly disease."[5]

As the courier traveled down the eastern seaboard toward the District of Columbia, the physician sailed back to Bermuda and set about amassing more soiled materials of the deceased. Among the items were "clothing, poultices, blankets and sheets, many stained with black vomit," according to the

New York Times, the latter feature being indicative of internal bleeding.[6] Secure in the knowledge that Hyams was unleashing the "yellow plague" on the East Coast, Blackburn was preparing the next phase of his grim project, that of disseminating it in northern metropolises. And topping his list would be the most populous of them all, New York City. He was banking on the outbreaks to distract and demoralize the citizens of the anti-slavery states, thereby sapping their resources and their resolve to continue waging war against the Confederacy.

As it came to pass, Blackburn's scheme would not proceed as planned. For one thing, Godfrey Hyams would not deliver the valise to the White House. Panic would seize him, the shoemaker realizing the consequences he would face if he were caught trying to pass the dread disease to Abraham Lincoln. For another, the clothing and other materials Blackburn had nicked from the Bermudian casualties did not, in fact, present a danger to the public. As Carlos Finlay, the Cuban physician and researcher, would discover a few years later, yellow fever is a mosquito-borne illness.

Because the insect vector had not yet been identified in 1864, however, Blackburn thought his clandestine offensive had struck one of its targets when the disease barreled through New Bern, North Carolina, in the autumn of that year. Counted as one the worst outbreaks in the country, Blackburn's only regret was that the Union soldiers occupying the town succumbed in smaller numbers than the townspeople themselves.[7] In all, over two thousand people perished in the horrific ordeal.

It would be seven months later that Abraham Lincoln joined the legions of the dead. And while he expired from an assassin's bullet rather than from Blackburn and Hyams' flawed attempt to fell him with yellow fever, this does not diminish the fact that the pair's scheme was immoral and unethical, especially as it was designed to also transmit the disease to the citizens of North Carolina and Virginia. "Their ignorance of infectious disease," writes Steers, "in no way mitigates their guilt in attempting to unleash biological warfare against civilian populations."[8] Similarly, it makes no difference that judicial authorities, upon learning of the plot to harm the president and believing the pair had caused the New Bern epidemic, allowed them to walk free owing to a legal technicality, or that Blackburn promptly resumed the practice of medicine and eventually was elected governor of Kentucky. As an attempt by American citizens to commit mass murder on American soil for wholly political purposes, the yellow fever plot was both unprecedented and unforgivable. But while the notion of using illness as a truncheon was rare in the New World—the British military's use of smallpox-tainted blankets to infect Native Americans in the 1700s stands as the principal exception—inflicting sickness as a means of gaining an edge over one's enemies was, in centuries past, anything but unique in other parts of the world. To date, historians have traced the practice back nearly five thousand years, and it is to these bygone times that we now turn our attention.

Pathogens in Antiquity

To begin our survey of the historical use of biological agents during periods of conflict, it will serve us well to review the basic terminology of the subject itself. "Biological warfare" (BW) refers to the use of living organisms, such as bacteria and fungi, to inflict harm on a human, animal, or plant population. Included are viruses, which most scientists consider to be nonliving entities, and which others, such as virologist Edward Rybicki, describe as hovering "at the edge of life."[9] Similar to biowarfare, and also touched upon in this survey, is "chemical warfare" (CW), which denotes the use of nonliving toxins to achieve the same ends. And lastly, "nuclear warfare" (NW) refers to the deployment of nuclear or thermonuclear devices for hostile purposes. Together, these three forms of assault constitute "weapons of mass destruction" (WMD), with each potentially capable of triggering what is known as a "mass casualty incident" (MCI). In some cases, an MCI, besides extracting a sizable human toll, may also produce large-scale property destruction and damage to the biosphere.[10] In terms of adapting a biological entity, chemical agent, or nuclear energy for such purposes, "weaponization" is the conventional term.

An early report of the latter process can be found in the ancient Chinese medical text, the *Pen-Ts'ao*.[11] Dating back to 2735 BCE, Shen Nung, a renowned herbalist and the founder of Chinese medicine, claimed that bands of Chinese warriors, while girding for battle, tipped their arrows with a deadly substance extracted from aconite, a flowering plant.[12] If Nung's account is accurate, it would make the use of contaminated arrows the oldest documented application of a toxin in wartime. As for the choice of aconite, it would have been ideal in battle since it is readily absorbed through the skin and kills right away, its victims falling ill shortly after exposure and succumbing to organ failure within a few hours of contact. Predictably, given the method's simplicity and potency, warriors and hunters on other continents came up with the poison-arrow idea as well, including the indigenous peoples of North and South America. Regarding the aconite plant itself, it acquired the nickname "wolfsbane" in some regions because of its expediency in eliminating wolves, among other predators.

In due course, and owing to regional differences in animal and plant life, additional agents were introduced into service in various parts of the world, among them curare, which produces paralysis, and a handful of substances extracted from amphibians.[13] In other cases, crude mixtures were concocted. Scythian warriors in 400 BCE, for instance, doused their spears in a blend of manure and blood before taking them into battle. If such a mixture was unavailable, the ferocious archers, renowned for their skill in waging war on horseback, would plunge their weapons into human cadavers before engaging an enemy.[14]

Of course, human nature being what it is, what happened next was perhaps inevitable and centered on the proliferation of hair-raising tales involving lethal-arrow attacks. In fact, this particular biowarfare practice gained such notoriety that it made its way into our language: the contemporary word *toxin* is derived from the Greek word *toxikon*, meaning "(poison for) arrows," according to the Oxford Dictionary.[15] The root word, *toxon*, refers to a bow and arrow.

Also traceable to antiquity is the military strategy of fouling the water supply of an enemy camp or territory. From what historians have been able to determine, the first incident of a mass poisoning of this sort took place during a battle in China in 559 BCE, when a military unit contaminated a portion of the Ching River.[16] A successful strategy, it managed to sicken the enemy soldiers without affecting the civilian population downstream, presumably because the river diluted the toxin. Historians further inform us that the region's armies did not resort to such untoward deeds on a regular basis. "Although denying water supplies became a fundamental tactic," writes Ralph Sawyer, "military writers still deemed poisoning water sources to be an unorthodox measure."[17]

One reason the scheme was relatively uncommon in China and elsewhere may stem from societal reactions to the practice itself: tainting a community's drinking water, like the use of other biological and chemical agents both then and now, was considered to be beneath contempt. Case in point: Ancient Greece in the succeeding century (431–404 BCE). At this time, the Spartan army contaminated the wells of its opponent, the Athenians, with this odious course of action leading to a mortality rate in the thousands.[18] But while the mass murder, in the short term, helped Sparta triumph over its challenger, the maneuver backfired in the long term by wrecking the Spartan army's reputation throughout the region.[19] The victors, it seems, were disparaged for having violated the rules of war, shifting the conflict from an honorable confrontation between soldiers on the battlefield to a dishonorable, covert assault on an unsuspecting and defenseless population.

Further historical cases include the Assyrians in 600 BCE, who contaminated their opponents' wells with ergot of rye, a fungus known for causing hallucinations, seizures, gangrene, and death, while Roman and Persian documents dating from 300 BCE reveal that soldiers tossed the remains of animals into enemy water supplies in an effort to spread disease.[20] Taking the measure a step further, soldiers in twelfth-century Italy disposed of the decomposing corpses of their fallen comrades by dumping them into their foes' water systems, again with contagion in mind.[21] And in nineteenth-century America, Confederate troops, as they were leaving Vicksburg, Mississippi, flung decaying animal carcasses into nearby ponds so as to make the water undrinkable for the Union troops who were bound to pursue them.[22]

As the centuries passed, an even more inventive form of germ warfare emerged and entailed the use of living animals. The earliest known application occurred in 1320–1318 BCE, in a region known as Anatolia in what is today the Republic of Turkey. During this period, two armies were embroiled in conflict, the Hittites and the Arzawans, with the former being the weaker force. Therefore, the Hittites, to gain an edge on their opponent, devised a clandestine scheme that entailed converting animals into weapons; in particular, animals sickened by the pathogen *Francisella tularensis*.[23] A bacterium, *F. tularensis* is transmitted mainly among hares, rabbits, and rodents, although humans may contract it through the bites of infected fleas, ticks, and deer flies, among other channels. And the result, a disease known as "tularemia," is potentially devastating. "Its symptoms range from skin ulcers, swollen and painful lymph glands to pneumonia, fever, chills, progressive weakness and respiratory failure," writes Rossella Lorenzi.[24] Molecular biologist Siro Trevisanato adds that tularemia was most likely the "Plague of the Philistines" as recounted in the Old Testament.[25]

As to how tularemia came to be a tool of biowarfare, it seems that a naturally-occurring outbreak of the illness was raging across Anatolia when the two armies went into battle, with the flurry of disease causing countless deaths as well as consternation in both military and civilian circles. And it was at this juncture that the Hittites, despite possessing no prior concept of bacterial infection, observed a connection between their ailing animals, chiefly rams and donkeys, and the sickness ravaging the area. Accordingly, they set about placing the afflicted beasts on the footpaths and roadways of the Kingdom of Arzawan, sometimes with herders to steer them through the countryside so as to spread the malady as far afield as possible. The Hittite's assumption, which turned out to be correct, was that the Arzawans would not suspect the listless creatures of being weapons of war.

By any standard, the exploitation of infected animals was an inspired idea, and it did, in fact, give the Hittites the upper hand in the conflict, if only for the moment. Either through an informer or simply by connecting the dots, the Arzawans soon discerned the relationship between the human scourge, the ailing rams and donkeys, and their Hittite enemy, and they promptly followed suit, releasing their own sickly animals into their adversary's territory. As could be expected, the epidemic worsened until the pestilence overwhelmed the entire region. As for the victor, ultimately it was the bacterium itself, which proved its worth as an instrument of biological assault.

Furthermore, owing to its effectiveness, it continued being used for such purposes for centuries to come. Even today, *F. tularensis* is on the shortlist of bacteria that experts consider the likeliest to be deployed in a biological attack.

Akin to the use of infected beasts to terrorize or kill an enemy, ancient militias also took advantage of the natural defenses of pernicious animals. A chilling example can be found in 190–184 BCE, during a confrontation between the forces of King Eumenes of Pergamon (Greece) and King Prusias of Bithynia in what is today north-central Turkey. It happened during a battle at sea, a lopsided showdown in which the Pergamonian fleet far outnumbered that of the Bithynian navy. To even the odds, the commander of the latter force, the brilliant strategist Hannibal Barca, resorted to an unheard-of tactic. An audacious scheme that would rely on the enemy's fear of pain and poison, it was, in effect, a fusion of psychological and biological warfare.

To put his idea into motion, Hannibal sent his men ashore with instructions to ensnare a batch of venomous snakes, pack them into earthenware pots, and return them to the Bithynian warships. Here, the clay vessels would be readied for the offensive. "Hannibal's idea was to terrorize Eumenes' crew so that they were unable to fight," writes Adrienne Mayor.[26]

When the moment arrived to deliver the payload, the Bithynians' method was crude but viable, with the seagoing soldiers hurling the clay vessels onto the decks of their adversaries' ships. And the action had the desired effect. "The enemy's first reaction to the smashing pottery was derisive laughter," writes Mayor, "[b]ut as soon as they realized their decks were seething with poisonous snakes … the horrified sailors leaped about trying to avoid the vipers."[27] As Hannibal had anticipated, the Pergamonians surrendered to panic and in so doing handed a victory to the Bithynian navy. The triumph did not come without a cost, though. As had happened in the past and would continue to occur in the future, the fact that biological elements had been introduced into the fight was viewed with contempt. "[I]t may have been this incident," says Mayor, "that led Eumenes to make his famous remark that an honorable general should eschew victory by underhanded means."[28]

Such controversial measures would persist, however, and would extend to other classes of animal. An illustrative case occurred during the same period in the desert fortress of Hatra, situated near the present-day city of Mosul, Iraq. Unlike Hannibal's assault, it did not involve reptiles, although the stand-in was just as unnerving and equally hazardous. The target was the invading legion of the Roman emperor Severus.

Determined to expand the Roman Empire's dominion into Mesopotamia, Severus, in 199–198 BCE, placed Hatra in its sights. Learning of his plans, the Hatreni soldiers who were posted at the stronghold set about preparing for battle, and to this end embarked upon the unenviable task of stuffing jars with what has been described as "poisonous winged insects."[29] Yet according to historians, the vessels held more than noxious bugs; they contained scorpions as well, an order of arachnids.[30] A practical source of ammunition in that scorpions were abundant in the desert surrounding the fortress, the tactic promised to disorient and debilitate the enemy.

A potentially lethal creature, the adult scorpion can reach up to eight inches in length, being roughly the size of a coffee cup, and has a segmented tail culminating in a barbed stinger. In the most dangerous species, its venom, which is comprised of several agents, neurotoxins among them, can produce seizures, paralysis, coma, respiratory failure, and cardiac arrest.

Confident the Roman forces rushing the fortress would be stopped in their tracks at the sight of the creatures, the Hatrenis, poised atop the fortress walls, dropped the jars onto the invaders at the outset of the attack. And the incursion came to a halt. Overcome with fright as the scorpion grenades rained down on them, the Romans turned tail, the result being that Hatra preserved its sovereignty and biological warfare chalked up another victory.

While additional types of animals and their toxins would serve as bioweapons in the years ahead—the Poles' use of a neurotropic virus found in the saliva of rabid dogs comes to mind—homo sapiens would eventually be weaponized, too, and not just in the form of corpses dropped into wells.[31] It would be in the 14th century, moreover, that the most appalling utilization of humans, truly toxic ones, would take place.

The Black Death, or bubonic plague, was thundering across the Far East at this time, on its way westward toward the Crimea. In its path was Kaffa, a Crimean port on the Black Sea, which the Republic of Genoa (Italy) was temporarily inhabiting by means of a pact with the seaport's owner, a Mongolian khanate known as the Golden Horde. Enjoying a strategic location, Kaffa constituted a vital nexus between East and West, serving as a departure point for trade caravans traversing the Silk Road to China while also offering considerable control over Black Sea trade routes. And it was this port city that the Genoese built into a lucrative trade colony. But as sometimes happens in such arrangements, a conflict arose between the Muslim Mongols and the Christian Genoese, with the disagreement intensifying until, in 1346, it turned bloody.[32] At this juncture, the Genoese administration in Kaffa decided to refuse entry to all Mongols, with the Mongols, for their part, refusing to be shut out of their own city and thus laying siege to it—this, as the Black Death was descending on the Crimean Peninsula. A "perfect storm" of sorts, conditions were ideal for the weaponization of the bacterium *Yersinia pestis*, the microorganism that causes the bubonic plague.

The strategy itself was imaginative, if macabre: the Mongols placed the corpses of plague victims onto catapults and propelled them over the city walls into Kaffa. Of course, the sight was not a pleasant one, nor was the scent. As the days passed and the human remains piled up, the stench pervaded the seaport, which is precisely what the Mongols had in mind. The process of infection not being understood at the time, the Golden Horde believed it was the odor of decomposing cadavers that caused the plague.[33] But while their theory about the disease's transmission was wrong, the Mongols' technique for deploying their human weapons was right on the mark, with Kaffa soon beset with the Black Death.

In terms of the plague's probable route of transmission, it has long been assumed that rats and other flea-carrying rodents in Kaffa gnawed on the corpses, then spread the disease to the seaport's denizens. A competing theory has recently been put forth, however, and it involves a more direct encounter with the source of *Y. pestis*. "Contact with tissue and blood," writes infectious disease specialist James Martin, "would have been inevitable during the disposal of hundreds or possibly thousands of cadavers that had been smashed on impact."[34] Whatever the avenue of transmission, the outbreak not only decimated Kaffa but also prompted scores of its residents to sail back to Italy, with the Black Death an unbidden passenger on this succession of voyages. Certainly it is true that, of the various mechanisms that have been proposed to account for the plague's arrival in medieval Europe, the bio-attack at Kaffa is a recurrent explanation. If correct, the ghoulish assault underscores a long-standing drawback of biological warfare, namely the difficulty its perpetrators face in controlling its impact. "[W]eapons that target human biological vulnerabilities are notoriously undiscriminating," writes Mayor.[35]

The unmanageable, even random, effects of biological warfare would come under better control in the 17th century, as European researchers made extraordinary advances in the medical sciences. Such revolutionary strides, while profoundly beneficial to humankind, also meant that practitioners of biowarfare could become better educated about disease and thus more able to fine-tune their delivery of it. Among the more important of these medical advances was the invention of the microscope, along with crucial enhancements to the device by the Dutch microbiologist Antonie van Leeuwenhoek. Further developments in the ensuing centuries came in the form of Robert Koch's groundbreaking bacteriological studies, Louis Pasteur's corroboration and advancement of germ theory, and Dmitri Ivanovsky and Martinus Beijerinck's discovery of viruses. Collectively, the breakthroughs of these and other scientists illuminated the mechanisms of such infections as anthrax, cholera, diphtheria, and tuberculosis; dreadful conditions that bio-warriors could now calibrate more precisely—meaning, in this context, less indiscriminately—against humanity.

Understandably, the prospect of a hostile nation misusing medical advances to commit mass murder alarmed many world leaders, the upshot being that several heads of state decided such atrocities should be prevented at all costs. And so they took action. "These dangers," writes Friedrich Frischknecht of the Institut Pasteur, "resulted in two international declarations—in 1874 in Brussels and in 1899 in the Hague—that prohibited the use of poisoned weapons."[36] Frischknecht adds, however, that these international agreements, while well-intentioned, contained no mechanisms for enforcement and were therefore impotent.[37] In effect, they were statements spelling out the signatories' moral position on biowarfare on the optimistic assumption that participating governments would abide by them. Yet this was not to happen. Biowarfare not only would persist, but escalate, most notably during the twentieth century.

Biological Warfare in the Modern Age

It was during World War I that Germany embarked on an ambitious germ warfare program, one that made use of the bacterium *Burkholderia mallei*, which causes glanders. A disease primarily of horses, the affliction in humans can produce chest pain, abscesses in the spleen and liver, pneumonia, and death, depending on the route of infection. Although postwar investigators failed to unearth irrefutable proof that the German military had, in fact, used this pathogen against its enemies—the defeated nation's scientists likely would have disposed of the incriminating evidence at war's end—it is believed that German operatives were sent into Romania to infect horses, mules, and sheep with the bacterium.[38] The animals were set to be exported to Russia, Germany's opponent in the war, and the expectation was that the contagious creatures would transmit the ailment to the Russian people. Saboteurs purportedly infected mules and horses in France with the same microorganisms, along with those in the United States.

Also during the conflict, the German military was said to have infected cattle with cholera and anthrax bacteria, even as that nation's scientists sought to convert a wheat fungus into a bioweapon.[39] And if these efforts were not enough to lay low its enemies, German technicians ostensibly devised a technique for spreading the bubonic plague, with the military attempting to introduce *Y. pestis* into Italy and Russia.[40]

Pathogenic agents, however, were not the only unconventional weapons employed by Germany. It also was the first nation in World War I to use toxic chemicals when it discharged chlorine gas onto the battlefield at Ypres, Belgium. Shrouding the landscape and descending into the adversaries' trenches, the heavy substance caused French, Canadian, and British soldiers to succumb to asphyxiation. In response, Germany's enemies adopted the same practice, such that, by war's end, the Central and Allied Powers had released hundreds of tons of poisonous chemicals, including not only chlorine gas but phosgene and mustard gas as well. As a direct result, well over a million men perished.

So menacing were Germany's suspected biological warfare activities, and so horrific were the chemical weapons' effects during the war, that the global community, during the interwar period, felt it necessary to formally address once again the issue of state-sponsored biochemical assaults. To this end, representatives from over a hundred nations gathered in Geneva, Switzerland, on June 17, 1925, to endorse a document titled the "Protocol for the Prohibition of the Use in War of Asphyxiating, Poisonous or Other Gases and of Bacteriological Methods of Warfare."[41] Known informally as the "Geneva Protocol of 1925," it was, like the two earlier pacts drawn up in the 1880s, intended to prevent the use of biologic weaponry. Yet, curiously, the 1925 version allowed the participating nations to continue stockpiling a range of pathogens, as well as continuing their research into this dubious form of warfare—provided, that is, they not deploy the results. The pact did not, however, require that their BW facilities be inspected, evidently on the assumption that the signatories could be trusted to honor the agreement. In reality, such vulnerabilities invited exploitation: while some nations, such as the United States, did not ratify the 1925 agreement—it would be another fifty years before the U.S. would do so—a handful of those that did endorse it soon violated the protocol, most conspicuously Japan.

Japan: Unit 731 (Manchuria)

It was during the 1930s that the civilian government of Japan found itself under the thumb of staunch militarists determined to transform their country into the world's frontrunner in biowarfare research and capability. It would be a development, the militarists argued, that would allow Japan to extend its borders. "They concluded that, because of its comparatively small population and limited natural resources, Japan could not achieve its expansionist objectives in East Asia unless it possessed weapons that could equalize the disparities with its rivals," writes Sheldon Harris in the *Annals of the New York Academy of Sciences*. "The militarists looked to biological warfare as a source of parity and recruited Japan's foremost scientists, physicians, dentists, veterinarians, and technicians to participate in the biological warfare program."[42]

In 1935, the classified project, under the auspices of the Imperial Army, commenced in Japanese-occupied Manchuria, with the setup being both wide-ranging and shocking in its inhumanity. Dubbed "Unit 731," the main complex was composed of over 150 buildings clustered in the remote town of Pingfan and surrounding villages. Comprised of eight major components, the Unit 731 divisions included a comprehensive bacteriological research center, along with a facility dedicated to the mass production of pathogenic agents and another that focused on water filtration systems. The purpose of the latter was to experiment with various methods of contaminating a country's waterworks. Perhaps the most ominous division, however, was the one in which the facility's medical staff intentionally infected healthy research subjects with either conventional pathogens or those that had been artificially enhanced, the purpose being to observe the microbes' courses of action.

Of course, a warfare program having the ambition of Unit 731 required a proportionate staff, and, indeed, the number of personnel at its central site was considerable. During the decade between its inception and its closure in 1945, Unit 731 counted among its employees three thousand scientists together with scores of medical professionals and biotechnicians. As to the research itself, Peter Williams and David Wallace, two former journalists presently affiliated with the BBC, detailed the massive project in their book *Unit 731: The Japanese Army's Secret of Secrets*.[43] Describing its overarching mission, the weaponization of bacteria, they write,

> Unit 731's bacteriological research division was divided into more than a dozen squads, each investigating the warfare possibility of a wide variety of diseases. Plague, anthrax, dysentery, typhoid, paratyphoid, cholera and many other exotic and unknown diseases were studied.... Various disease vectors, mainly insect, were investigated, as were new drugs, chemical toxins and frostbite.[44]

Unit 731's pool of research subjects was another feature that the program's architects took to extremes. It set a precedent, in fact, in that it not only used human beings as guinea pigs but also killed untold numbers of them after exposing them to experimental microorganisms so the staff could autopsy the corpses and observe the pathogens' effects. Also disturbing, the dissections were often performed without anesthesia, with the victims fully conscious. "If we'd used anesthesia, that might have affected the body organs and the blood vessels that we were examining," says a present-day farmer who served as a medic at the facility.[45] In its disregard for human life, Unit 731 anticipated the Nazis' brutal medical experiments that would be conducted in the succeeding years at Auschwitz, Bergen-Belsen, and other concentration camps.

Regarding the research subjects' characteristics, many were Chinese prisoners-of-war, along with a smaller portion of Russian POWs, with over three thousand such captives perishing at the hands of the scientists.[46] An even larger number of casualties—seven thousand Japanese citizens—were drawn from more conventional circumstances, the majority of whom were either political dissidents or run-of-the-mill lawbreakers. And then there were those who had not offended the government in any way. "Unsuspecting and innocent people were also tricked into the clutches of Unit 731," write

Williams and Wallace. "Young boys, mothers and children, even pregnant women, were trapped."[47] Some were led to believe they were being hired for an unspecified task only to find themselves confined in the bowels of a government building in Harbin, a Japanese-occupied city in northeastern China. In due course, they would be spirited away to Unit 731 under cover of darkness in convoys composed of windowless trucks.[48] Awaiting them would be disease and death, occasionally in the form of artificially-induced mini-epidemics in which small numbers of research subjects would be injected with pathogens, then inserted into larger groups of healthy individuals so investigators could study the ensuing outbreaks' patterns of spread.

Besides the research carried out in Unit 731's laboratories, the staff also conducted field studies. In these experiments, human subjects were herded to a secret testing ground, strapped to poles, and exposed to toxins dispersed by means of an aerial procedure similar to crop dusting. Alternatively, rolling vehicles were used to distribute the pathogens at ground level. In all cases, the aim was to formulate delivery systems that would ensure fast and fierce epidemics. When such experiments yielded positive results, the Unit 731 staff, via the Imperial Army, would target the Chinese population using the new methods.

In one offensive of this type, Japanese soldiers, overseen by Unit 731 scientists, released plague-carrying animals into China, with the bio-attack producing an estimated thirty thousand civilian casualties.[49] In other actions, troops spiked the water and food supplies of diverse Chinese cities, sparking outbreaks of typhoid, cholera, and dysentery.

Perhaps the most sinister, however, was Unit 731's creation of disease bombs. To devise these innovative weapons, Japanese scientists packed healthy fleas into sealed chambers that held animal carcasses infected with bubonic plague. Since no other food source was available, the insects fed on the diseased remains and in this way acquired the *Y. pestis* bacterium. Subsequent to this, technicians placed the infected fleas into containers, an estimated fifteen million per "plague bomb," and released them from low-flying aircraft over Chinese cities. And, as anticipated, the targets were soon beset with the deadly illness. Hardest hit was the city of Changteh, where ten thousand people expired along with nearly two thousand Japanese soldiers who were likewise exposed during the blanket dissemination of the pathogen.[50] Yet the high mortality rate of its troops did not spur the Japanese military to pare down its attacks on China or, for that matter, to limit its offensives to Asia: there is reason to believe Japan may have been planning a similar assault on the United States, according to the *New York Times*.[51]

It was 1944 and the Christmas holidays were approaching, but for some Americans it was not the seasonal festivities that were drawing their attention but rather the unusual balloons that had begun touching down in their neighborhoods. So they did what any concerned citizen would do under the circumstances. They phoned the authorities.

At first, the calls came from residents of San Diego, California, and Butte, Montana, but over the next three months they also poured in from the Aleutian Islands, Hawaii, Alaska, Michigan, and parts of Canada.[52] As to the balloons' origins, military officials concluded they had been dispatched from Japan owing to their construction—they were made of rice paper and silk— and because the prevailing winds would have carried them eastward to the west coast of the United States and Canada. It was, to be sure, a harrowing development, especially since the inflatables were equipped with metal boxes that contained incendiary devices. Stunned, the government decided to withhold all information about the "balloon bombs" from the public—not even a mention in passing—so as to dissuade Japan from releasing more, and possibly enhanced, versions of them. "[T]he Office of Censorship" writes Jeffrey Alan Smith, "asked American news organizations not to report on their existence so that the enemy would be deprived of information on their effectiveness."[53]

As it stood, the preponderance of balloons, nine thousand in all, failed to make it across the Pacific Ocean. Only two hundred survived the high-altitude journey. Furthermore, those that did reach the North American continent turned out to be worthless, with nearly all of their bombs failing to detonate. The few that did ignite, however, brought dire consequences. Half a dozen civilians, not knowing the balloons' metal boxes housed explosive devices, were killed when they pried them open, among the casualties being a Montana woman and a group of Sunday School children in Oregon. It was because of such incidents that the U.S. government eventually lifted the media blackout; the public needed to know the inflatables posed a danger of detonation.[54] What the public would not be told is that officials also worried that the balloons might be carrying biological agents.

Of foremost concern was the potential release of the encephalitis or yellow fever viruses, neither of which the U.S. was equipped to contain at epidemic levels. Driving this fear, military intelligence knew the Japanese had recently tried to procure the yellow fever pathogen from sources in three different countries. Accordingly, the military sent its personnel to recover the balloons' remnants for analysis, this at a time when the state of biohazard protection was still rather rudimentary. "Pathetic-sounding precautions were listed," write Williams and Wallace, with those retrieving the potentially toxic balloons being instructed to don gloves and gas masks and to tie their pant legs at the ankle—certainly not the securest of measures.[55] As it turned out, they needn't have worried, since the military's scientists ultimately concluded that the inflatables were free of pathogens.

Understandably, Japan's decision not to outfit the balloons with biological agents mystified American military scientists. One hypothesis centered on the notion that Japan was reluctant to ignite a biological confrontation, an explanation supported in part by the words of a Japanese official after the war. "Hideki Tojo," writes Smith, "the politician and military leader who was later hanged for war crimes, rejected the idea [of a bio-attack] as too likely to bring germ or chemical retaliation from the United States."[56] Lieutenant Colonel Murray Sanders, formerly a member of the United States' chemical warfare program, offered another possibility. "The only explanation I had, and still have, is that [Unit 731 Director] Ishii wasn't ready to deliver what he was making in Pingfan; that he hadn't worked out the technology."[57]

It would be this same Japanese microbiologist, Shirō Ishii, the Allies would decide not to prosecute for war crimes when the opportunity presented itself at the end of the conflict. Rather, the United States would strike a deal with him whereby Ishii would share the findings of Unit 731's unscrupulous research program with American scientists in exchange for immunity from prosecution.[58] In a scathing essay, *An Ethical Blank Cheque*, Cambridge University historian Richard Drayton notes that Ishii not only handed over his research results to the Americans but also traveled to the U.S. government's secret biological warfare program in Maryland, presumably Camp Detrick, to serve as an advisor.[59]

United States: Camp Detrick

Originally known as Detrick Field, the site that would become America's premiere biowarfare facility began rather modestly as a regional airstrip named in honor of Frederick L. Detrick, a flight surgeon for the Maryland National Guard. In 1943, at the height of World War II, the Army's Chemical Warfare Service acquired the spot, renamed it Camp Detrick, and transformed it into a state-of-the-art biowarfare research complex.[60] And scientific inquiry flourished. Under the leadership of pharmaceutical tycoon George Merck and bacteriologist Ira Baldwin, Camp Detrick set about amassing an array of microbial agents for study, with the endeavor accelerating during the Cold War as the staff braced for an East-West confrontation. "For two decades beginning in the late 1940s," reports the *Washington Post*, "it led the U.S. government's efforts to research and develop biological weapons."[61]

By any index, Camp Detrick, at its zenith, was impressive. "[T]here [were] some 200 separate projects under way at the post," writes Ed Regis, "everything from anthrax spore production to the mass cultivation of killer mosquitoes to research on the dissemination of plant diseases such as late blight of potatoes."[62] In the mid–1800s, it had been this same "late blight," a fungal condition, that brought about the devastating Irish potato famine. Clearly, the Detrick operation was determined to be both inventive and far-reaching. To achieve its lofty aims, moreover, it ensured that it had an abundance of staff, counting among its researchers many of the U.S. military's top figures in the life sciences. "At peak strength, 2,273 people were working at Camp Detrick, including 1,702 Army personnel, 562 Navy, and 9 civilians."[63] Despite the size of the operation, however, details of its activities were as rigorously concealed from the public as those of another wartime undertaking, the Manhattan Project.

"Secrecy was always an uppermost consideration at Detrick, and people working in one lab building were prohibited from talking about their jobs with those in the next lab, or, indeed, with anyone else," says Regis. "To ensure compliance, the Army stationed spies in the barracks to eavesdrop on conversations and report infractions."[64] Yet such tight security was warranted; certainly it would have been a coup for the United States' adversaries to gain access to the facility's research projects. And the secrecy served another function as well, shielding the Camp Detrick program from the eyes an American public that would have been taken aback by the classified research being carried out by the facility's staff at undisclosed locations across the homeland.

Compared to the earlier BW activities of German and Japanese scientists, those of American researchers were generally in line with the recognized ethical standards of the day. Citing the need for secrecy, however, Detrick scientists occasionally conducted studies without the knowledge or consent of the participants. Today, these same investigations, which involved exposure to microbial agents, would not pass muster with oversight committees. But in the mid-twentieth century, the United States was in the grip of the Cold War, survival was foremost in the minds of the Detrick staff, and ethical criteria were still evolving.

Of the studies carried out on the unsuspecting public, perhaps the most dubious ones were those involving the dissemination of biological agents in highly-populated regions. Such studies, researchers explained, were intended to bring about a better understanding of the process by which a foreign military, using airborne pathogens, could contaminate a sizable swath of the American population; information that would help the Detrick staff more effectively prepare the nation to weather such an attack. As for the methodology, a newly-established unit at the facility, the "Secret Operations Division," decided the most effective means of studying the large-scale release of pathogenic agents would entail staging a series of bio-attacks of its own, albeit benign ones.

In this unprecedented undertaking, the Pentagon, the nerve center of the U.S. Department of Defense, was the first to be targeted. Here in the summer of 1949, Detrick operatives disguised as maintenance workers strolled through the thirty-four acre structure releasing the microorganism *Serratia marcescens*. A bacterium, *S. marcescens* is infrequently associated with respiratory and urinary tract infections, meningitis, pneumonia, and other afflictions, but six decades ago it was not known to be pathogenic to humans. For this reason, the Detrick team used the microorganism as a stand-in for the more lethal ones the nations' foes could be expected to employ during an actual attack.

In terms of its dispersal, the operatives discharged the germ from suitcases equipped with air pumps and spouts, spraying *S. marcescens* in the corridors as well as directly into the ventilation system.[65] And the outcome of the experiment was revealing: the building's air-purification process was incapable of preventing the microorganism from traveling throughout the sprawling structure. Without doubt, it was an important finding, and one that the team obtained rather easily by tracking the bright red pigment, "prodigiosin," that characterized the strain of *S. marcescens* used in the investigation. (Parenthetically, it was because of the microorganism's crimson color, which gives it a blood-like appearance, coupled with the fact that it is sometimes found in starchy foods, such as bread, that *S. marcescens* is thought to have been the source of Medieval transubstantiation miracles in which blood was believed to materialize on communion bread as it was being transmuted into the body of Christ during the Eucharist.[66])

In April 1950, Detrick scientists used the same red microorganism in a second experiment as well as adding *Bacillus globigii* to the mix, another entity thought to be innocuous. Only several years later would it be determined that it, too, is potentially harmful to humans. In the mid-twentieth century, however, when *B. globigii* was still considered safe, it was often employed as a simulant in germ warfare research because it shares certain properties with the anthrax bacterium.

The experiment itself took place aboard two Navy vessels situated off the coast of Virginia. The objective was to trace the movement of *S. marcescens* and *B. globigii* when released from the sea; specifically, from the decks of a destroyer and an aircraft carrier. And the results were daunting. It seems the wind carried the microorganisms to the coastal cities of Norfolk and Newport News, Virginia, and it did so swiftly and in significant quantities.

Building on this study five months later, scientists used aerosolized forms of *S. marcescens* and *B. globigii* in a much grander scheme, namely a mock attack on the city of San Francisco. In this unique—and once again, undisclosed—experiment, researchers sprayed batches of the two microorganisms from a brace of Navy minesweepers positioned off the San Francisco Peninsula.[67] As part of the investigation, they also released fluorescent particles into the atmosphere, because such material, being readily detectable using ultraviolet light, can be easily tracked. And sure enough, the fluorescent material was detected up to twenty-five miles in the interior of California, with each of San Francisco's 800,000 residents having inhaled an estimated five thousand particles.[68] The findings further suggested that the *S. marcescens* and *B. globigii* had reached the metropolitan area as well.

To be sure, the ethics of the San Francisco study were problematical, yet the results themselves were informative. Their value, however, was limited by the experiment's focus on the Bay Area, meaning the findings were not necessarily applicable to other regions. Researchers therefore set about conducting additional studies in an effort to understand microbial distribution patterns in other locations, including such congested venues as the New York City subway system and Washington National Airport. "[T]he Detrick scientists would end up performing more than 200 simulant trials in, around, or upon the United States, sparing no corner of the country," writes Regis.[69] As before, those directly impacted by the experiments, the American people, would not know they were, in effect, serving as the human equivalent of lab rats.

Regarding Camp Detrick's fate, the government deemed it a permanent fixture in 1956 and christened it Fort Detrick. But although the new name would remain in place, the site's activities would change thirteen years later when President Richard Nixon, under pressure from American scientists and members of Congress, called a halt to the government's research into offensive biowarfare. "Our bacteriological programs in the future will be confined to research in biological defense, on techniques of immunization, and on measures on controlling and preventing the spread of disease," Nixon declared.[70] Thereafter, Fort Detrick became the facility it is today, home to a variety of medical research centers, among them a branch of the National Cancer Institute and the U.S. Army Medical Research Institute of Infectious Diseases (USAMRIID). Fort Detrick also houses a sophisticated biodefense research center.

Here it should be noted that the United States was not alone in possessing a BW program. Other nations were pursuing such research as well, and not just investigations aimed at formulating treatment protocols in response to an attack. In some countries, they also involved the aggressive use of pathogens.

Canada, for instance, initiated such a program in the 1940s, one developed under the leadership of orthopedic surgeon and researcher Sir Frederick Banting, recipient of the Nobel Prize in 1923 for his pioneering work in extracting insulin from the pancreas for use in the management of diabetes. It seems that Banting, whose contributions to medicine have saved untold lives, was not averse to using his brilliance to take lives as well. During World War II, he became an outspoken advocate of retaliating against—that is to say, eliminating through disease—Germans, or "huns" as he called them. He believed such a response would be fitting if Germany were to first attack the Allies with biological weapons.

"It is time that the old school tie was ironed free of wrinkles & folded up & put in a box until this show is over," the Nobel laureate writes in his diary. "We have to kill 3 or 4 million young huns—without mercy—without feeling."[71]

The Canadian government subsequently granted Banting permission to set up a biowarfare program to be coordinated with those of Britain and the United States. "This would eventually lead to the production and testing of anthrax munitions in Canada," writes Albert Mauroni, Director of the U.S. Air Force Center of Unconventional Weapons Studies.[72]

USSR: Biopreparat

While Canada's cultivation of anthrax bacteria represented a stark departure for the peaceable nation, the size and scope of its enterprise paled in comparison to that of the Soviet Union, the final national biowarfare program to be revisited in this historical survey. Characterized by a plethora of secret studies conducted on the USSR's human, animal, and plant populations, the Soviet program proved to be one of the most extensive and advanced BW endeavors of the twentieth century.

Harking back to 1928, the USSR began by attempting to weaponize *Rickettsia prowazekii*, the bacterium that causes typhus. Scientists, a decade earlier, had watched helplessly as a natural-occurring outbreak of the disease delivered suffering and death to the masses, and, in due course, decided the pathogen might make a formidable weapon for use on the battlefield. To this end, they sought to liquefy *R. prowazekii*, as well aerosolize it, a project that continued for the next two decades.

Typhus, however, was just the beginning. The communist state's program made a quantum leap forward near the end of World War II, when Soviet soldiers, upon liberating Manchuria, discovered their foe's abandoned biowarfare center. Here, at Unit 731, troops gathered up blueprints of the facility, research protocols, and other materials, and handed them over to military intelligence for use in interrogating Japanese scientists being held at prisoner-of-war camps. And the next step was predictable: Josef Stalin, awed by the scope of the Japanese undertaking, ordered a Soviet version to be created. It was in this way that the USSR's comprehensive biowarfare operation came into existence, one that soon eclipsed its Asian predecessor. And it continued to expand, most dramatically in 1973 with the formation of "Biopreparat," an agency comprised of an assembly of experts whose role was to furnish scientific and engineering know-how for secret-weapons projects.

Between 1988 and 1991, Kanatzhan Alibekov, a prominent microbiologist and physician, served as Biopreparat's deputy director. After defecting to the United States in 1992, he adopted the name Ken Alibek and penned an account of his days at the agency, a text titled *Biohazard*.[73] In it, he revisited the work performed at Biopreparat's numerous research and production facilities dating back to its inception, calling special attention to its efforts to engineer outbreaks of such bacterial illnesses as anthrax, brucellosis, glanders, plague, and tularemia. Depicting the staff as single-minded and inventive, Alibek further recounted how Biopreparat's scientists enjoyed boundless funding while pursuing research at its state-of-the-art sites; sites boasting laboratories that were, to say the least, well-stocked. Whereas other nations cultivated small amounts of pathogens for biowarfare research, the size of the Soviets' stockpiles was jaw-dropping. "Target capacity" writes Alibek, "[was] up to 100 tons of each weapon annually."[74]

Yet there was more to Biopreparat than its overarching interest in conventional bacterial outbreaks. With the cooperation of the Ministry of Agriculture, it mass-produced anti-crop weapons, along with anti-livestock agents aimed at killing cows, chickens, and pigs. Scientists at the Institute of Molecular Biology, meanwhile, sought to create novel pathogens by genetically altering viruses as well as by combining components of multiple agents. And elsewhere in the USSR, researchers brainstormed innovative methods of dispensing pathogens, including the use of cruise missiles, or "biocruises."

But even as the Biopreparat staff worked with known bacteria and viruses, including those that cause Bolivian hemorrhagic fever, Ebola, human and equine encephalitis, Marburg hemorrhagic fever, and smallpox, researchers also kept abreast of newly discovered pathogens and explored their feasibility as weapons of mass destruction. Foremost among them was *Legionella pneumophila*, a bacterium identified in 1976 and the causative agent of Legionnaire's Disease, a form of pneumonia. Another was the human immunodeficiency virus (HIV), identified in 1983 and the lentivirus responsible for AIDS. In the end, though, Soviet researchers concluded that the two pathogens, as potential biological warfare agents, were too unstable for use in the theater of war or against civilian populations. In the case of the latter microbe, there was another reason as well.

"After studying one strain of the AIDS virus collected from the United States in 1985, we determined that HIV's long incubation period made it unsuitable for military use," says Alibek. "You couldn't strike terror in an enemy's forces by infecting them with a disease whose symptoms took years to develop."[75] Undaunted, Biopreparat scientists continued to pursue methods of compromising the human immune system—until, that is, all of agency's endeavors ended unceremoniously in 1991 with the collapse of the Soviet Union and its replacement by a collection of autonomous states. Although Biopreparat's activities ceased at this juncture, however, the threat of a bio-attack lingered. Only the players would change.

"In 1992," writes political scientist Leonard Cole, "Russian President

Boris Yeltsin acknowledged that the former Soviet Union had developed tons of anthrax, plague, and other forbidden warfare agents."[76] A startling admission by the new head of state, political leaders around the world respected his candor. That said, Yeltsin's unexpected disclosure raised troubling questions about the future destination of the former USSR's stockpiles of pathogens, with many observers fearing the microbes might find their way into the hands of terrorists. A distressing prospect, it is a worry that persists today, the concern that bio-weapons, historically the province of nations' militaries, may be purchased or perhaps manufactured by autonomous extremist groups. To be sure, this represents a perilous turning point in the arena of biowarfare, since it means the deliberate use of pathogens to inflict widespread harm, always a danger, has become even more unpredictable.

Bioterrorism

The apprehension that a terrorist organization might acquire biological weapons was validated in 1995 when the Aum Shinrikyo group, a Japanese doomsday cult, conducted an attack on Tokyo's subway system. In the wake of this crime, which used the highly toxic, fast-acting nerve gas sarin to kill over a dozen commuters and injure a thousand more, investigators stormed the perpetrators' compound and discovered sophisticated chemical and biological warfare laboratories. In the latter, forensic analyses revealed that the cult's members had been conducting research on the Ebola virus and the anthrax bacterium, among other pathogens. This revelation did not come as a surprise to the authorities, however; the group had earlier attempted to discharge bacterial agents from atop a skyscraper and toxic gas from a specially-equipped van. What the subway attack did demonstrate is that biochemical weapons were no longer the sole possession of nations but were expanding into non-state, terrorist circles, and that such agents could cause substantial physical harm and considerable societal disturbance.

While several definitions of terrorism have been proposed over the years, each underscoring different dimensions of the phenomenon, the Department of Defense has issued perhaps the most widely cited one: "The unlawful use of violence or threat of violence, often motivated by religious, political, or other ideological beliefs, to instill fear and coerce governments and societies in pursuit of goals that are usually political."[77] Bioterrorism, in particular, pursues such ends through the use of toxins and infectious agents to debilitate or kill human, animal, or plant populations. As to its impact, it tends to be gauged qualitatively. "The success of bioterrorist attempts is defined by the measure of societal disruption and panic, and not necessarily by the sheer

number of casualties," writes Hugo-Jan Jansen, senior advisor at the Netherlands' Ministry of Defense.[78]

In 1998, the White House became so concerned about the sudden rise
in anthrax incidents in the United States—the number jumped from one
episode in 1997 to thirty-seven in 1998—that President Bill Clinton issued
two directives calling for federal agencies to enhance the nation's ability to
respond to such threats.[79] This led to the 1999 Bioterrorism Initiative, which
assigned to the Centers for Disease Control and Prevention the task of
upgrading the nation's capacity to respond to a bio-assault through a set of
coordinated public health protocols. Sweeping by design, the procedures inte-
grated the activities of both non-governmental and governmental agencies
at the federal, state, and local levels, and were welcomed by experts in the
field as a resourceful plan of action in the event of a large-scale assault. Suffice
it to say, the White House would have taken even more stringent action had
it known what al-Qaeda was contemplating at precisely this moment.

The al-Qaeda Anthrax Project

The global terrorist organization al-Qaeda, established in 1988, was created to repel what it regarded as an uninvited foreign influence in Islamic
lands, most notably the intrusiveness of the United States. The group also
sought to derail or destroy those regional Islamic regimes it judged to be cor-
rupt.

After relocating the organization's headquarters to Afghanistan in 1996,
its leader, Osama bin Laden, doubled down on his determination to fulfill
this two-fold mission, and to this end directed his strategists to pursue more
sensational forms of political intimidation. In time, this would come to
include not only al-Qaeda's meticulously choreographed, telegenic attack on
the World Trade Center, but also its quest to attain weapons of mass destruction. "[I]f I seek to acquire these weapons," declared bin Laden in an interview
with *Time* magazine, "I am carrying out a [religious] duty."[80]

Pushing ahead, the al-Qaeda leader ordered his deputy, the former surgeon Ayman al-Zawahiri, to organize and oversee a WMD program with
nuclear, chemical, and biological capabilities. Al-Zawahiri, in turn, brought
into the fold Rauf Ahmed, a microbiologist with the Pakistan Council of Scientific and Industrial Research, and Mohammad Atif, chief of al-Qaeda's Military Committee, to help manage the latter two components. And so it began.

In mid–1999, the team launched a project code-named "al Zabadi," an
Arabic term meaning "curdled milk."[81] As one of its early efforts, researchers
concocted what has been described as an insecticide-based, "home-brew
nerve gas," which they tested on rabbits and stray dogs at a field camp in the
Afghanistan desert.[82] The team also explored the chemical mixture napalm,

essentially a gelled form of gasoline that, when ignited, adheres to the skin and causes potentially fatal fourth-degree burns. And side-by-side with their interest in these and other crude chemical and incendiary methods was a preoccupation with weaponizing biological agents, with this presenting a further set of challenges for the team.[83]

In a persuasive letter to his superiors, Rauf Ahmed, after attending a conference titled "Dangerous Pathogens 2000" in England and touring a biosafety lab in that same country, insisted that al-Qaeda needed to entice more specialists from academic institutions if it hoped to build a robust WMD program. And the missive identified another need as well.[84] According to a précis published by the Combating Terrorism Center at West Point, Ahmed made the case that "a cover-up for the program would be needed, such as by setting up an NGO [non-governmental organization], private company, teaching institute or medical laboratory."[85]

As advised, al-Qaeda promptly attempted to recruit additional scientists and ensure that their activities had sufficient cover. The organization's biological and chemical warfare program also acquired new categories of stock, among them the bacteria *Clostridium botulinum* and *Salmonella* as well as the chemical compound cyanide. Presumably, the plan was to expose American troops in the region to the bacteria, and perhaps to the cyanide as well. "Botulism or salmonella poisoning would kill relatively few healthy young men or women," writes Pulitzer Prize-winning journalist Barton Gellman, "but would disable many of them for a time and render them vulnerable to other forms of attack."[86] Gellman adds that it would have been feasible for al-Qaeda to contaminate the soldiers' food, since local civilians prepared some of the meals.[87]

Perhaps most disconcerting, though, was the organization's fascination with anthrax. In November 2001, when members of the U.S.-led coalition stormed into Afghanistan in response to al-Qaeda's September 11th attack, they discovered a trove of bioterrorism materials in a nondescript house in an upscale neighborhood of Kabul, the capital city. The home of nuclear engineer Sultan Bashiruddin Mahmood, top al-Qaeda figures, among them al-Zawahiri himself, had been using the second floor as a meeting place to brainstorm WMD scenarios.

Scattered throughout were gas masks, laboratory equipment, and training manuals, along with booklets suggesting that an anthrax seminar had recently been conducted at the site. On hand, too, were materials detailing the U.S. military's plan to vaccinate its troops against the bacterium, along with an article about the Plum Island research facility in the United States, formerly a component of the nation's secret biowarfare program. Most telling, though, was a series of illustrations sketched on a wall. "The diagrams, in black marker pen, [were] detailed and esoteric, with pictures of helium balloons rising on carefully measured trajectories of 10 kilometers, then apparently being shot down by a jet fighter," writes Chris Stephen.[88] The organization seemed to be toying with the idea of tricking the United States into using its own military aircraft to detonate anthrax bombs in much the same way that al-Qaeda strategists had used the United States' domestic airliners to bring down the World Trade Center.

Following another foray in 2002, this one near an airport in the Afghanistan city of Kandahar, coalition forces came across a partially-completed laboratory that al-Qaeda members had abandoned in the wake of the devastating air raids in the region. When the military's technicians analyzed the site, they detected the tell-tale traces of anthrax.[89] A disturbing finding, it would be corroborated in 2003 with the capture of Khalid Sheik Mohammed, the principal architect of the September 11th attacks. Found hiding in the home of a retired microbiologist in Pakistan, a special ops team seized the al-Qaeda mastermind along with his notebooks and numerous other items. While all of the confiscated materials proved to be enlightening, it was his computer hard-drive that was most incriminating, containing, as it did, invoices for anthrax, inventories of pathogens, and timelines for the construction of biological and chemical weapons.[90] As American experts had suspected, the existence of such documents confirmed that al-Qaeda was still considering the use of biochemical agents against the United States and its allies.

Significantly, it was this same year, 2003, that an al-Qaeda cell from Bahrain, having formulated a cyanide-based gas which it dubbed the "mobtaker," prepared to release the substance on the New York City subway system.[91] The attack, however, would not be completed. Ayman al-Zawahiri, who learned about the plot at the eleventh hour, intervened at once, commanding the cell's members to abort the mission and return to the Arabian Peninsula. And his reason for doing so speaks volumes about the al-Qaeda mindset. "Zawahiri canceled the planned attack on the New York City subway for 'something better,'" says Rolf Mowatt-Larssen of the Harvard Kennedy School of Government, "suggesting that a relatively easy attack utilizing tactical weapons would not achieve the goals the al Qaeda leadership had set for themselves."[92] The attack, in other words, would not have been sensational enough to advance the organization's global reputation. After the September 11th pageant of destruction, al-Qaeda appears to have decided its forthcoming missions should be ever more spectacular, the organization having raised its own bar. To date, it has not staged a successful biological assault, presumably because the group still has not achieved the necessary expertise.

In an appraisal of al-Qaeda's bioweapons program, including its various anthrax projects, terrorism experts René Pita and Rohan Gunaratna report that the organization has experienced only limited success in its efforts, a state of affairs they attribute largely to its inability to recruit scientists having the necessary contacts.[93] Despite repeated attempts, the group has not been able to enlist researchers, such as those in Indonesia, who enjoy access to their homelands' reserves of pathogens.[94] This does not mean, however, that al-Qaeda will fail to attract well-connected figures in the future, nor does it rule out the possibility that the organization or another such group will secure a state sponsor that will supply it with WMDs or the tools for developing them. "Due to such sponsorship," writes Jeffrey Simon, formerly of the RAND Corporation, "[a terrorist group] could easily be provided with the necessary training, resources, and weapons."[95] Such a possibility is obviously a cause for concern.

As this chapter has revealed, humanity's propensity for inflicting illness upon its own kind is a practice that is as long-standing as it is reprehensible. Unfortunately, it is also one that shows no sign of abating. And worsening matters, the characteristics of those who engineer and execute biological assaults are expanding to include outlying elements of society that are at once atypical and unpredictable. Whereas in previous centuries it was most often a nation's military that developed and deployed biological agents, today's bio-warriors have come to include extremists, be they members of structured organizations or so-called "lone wolf" actors operating wholly on their own. In virtually every case, moreover, their targets are the same: civilian populations.

Disconcerting, too, is the fact that bio-attacks staged by terrorists are increasingly likely to succeed due to advances in society itself. The accessibility of international air travel, the expedited communication offered by the Internet, and the profound leaps taking place in such fields as genetic engineering, or "gene editing," are but a few of the developments that may help to facilitate terrorists' cultivation and dissemination of pathogens.

"While predicting … an attack with certainty is not possible," writes biodefense strategist Daniel Gerstein, "we must understand the proliferation of technology, increasing connectedness of the world, and a propensity toward more-spectacular attacks suggests the probability of such a large-scale bioterror attack will increase in the future."[96] The prospect of a sweeping bio-assault is, of course, appalling. It is also one society must address if it is to protect itself from those discontented individuals who conspire to destabilize it by unleashing a biological catastrophe.

◆ 2 ◆

Bioterrorism and Biocrime
Ideologies, Motives and Objectives

Terrorists and their organizations, including those that are inclined to use biological agents in their attacks, are not a uniform lot. They diverge in several respects, from the motives that drive their aggression to the scale of public exposure they hope to gain from their actions. In terms of size and complexity, they also run the gamut, from solitary extremists—so-called *lone wolves*—to outsized transnational organizations, just as their offensives range from hastily-staged, one-off attacks to well-orchestrated and prolonged campaigns of violence.

In the pages that follow, five broad categories of terrorism are examined, with special attention to those that experts believe are the likeliest to use microbial pathogens and biological toxins in their offensives. Discussed, too, is the less sensational but nonetheless significant realm of biocrime, which again entails the use of biological agents to commit misdeeds, albeit in a more personal vein. The aim is to furnish an overview of the types of organizations and individuals that are drawn to biological violence, as well as their aspirations in employing living organisms as an alternative to more conventional weapons.

Types of Terrorism

It was during the French Revolution that the term "terrorism" was coined, and, at that time in the eighteenth century, it carried a positive meaning. "Terror is nothing but prompt, severe, inflexible justice," writes Maximilien Robespierre in his 1794 treatise, *Justification of the Use of Terror*. "[I]t is therefore an emanation of virtue."[1] Robespierre was defending the bloody actions of France's revolutionary government, specifically its "Reign of Terror" as it came to be known in English-speaking nations. Touted as both honorable

30

and patriotic, the new government's deeds consisted of executing tens of thousands of citizens, aristocrats among them, who were judged to be hampering its seizure of power and, in some cases, conspiring to undermine it. The first casualty: Marie Antoinette, whom the new leadership sent to the guillotine.

Since those bygone days, terrorism has come to be defined quite differently, as an unnecessarily destructive approach to social or political change, as well as one that is adopted mostly by non-state actors. Society also views it in a profoundly dishonorable light. In fact, it is almost universally rejected except by those who engage in it and therefore strain to construe it as morally justifiable. This is perhaps most visibly the case for those religious extremists who claim that violence not only is supported by their belief systems, but is in fact necessary to advance their ideologies.

Religious Extremism

Jerrold Post, professor and director of the Political Psychology Program at George Washington University, has compiled a list of several types of terrorism, with religious extremism comprising one of the most lethal in terms of the total number of casualties.

"Religious-extremist terrorism is characterized by groups seeking to maintain or create a religious social and political order," writes Post, a system founded on "a radical fundamentalist interpretation of mainstream religious doctrines, including Islam, Judaism, Christianity, and Sikhism."[2] In such a group, the membership places its faith in a central figure, typically a cleric-leader operating outside the norm and claiming to speak for God, and it reveres this leader's directives which are purportedly based on scripture. Unfortunately, such directives call for violence against those who do not share the group's goal of the establishment of a fundamentalist society. "The radical cleric, whether ayatollah, rabbi, or priest, may draw on sacred text to justify killing in the name of God."[3] It should be noted that such groups, owing to their attraction to mass-casualty scenarios, may choose to kill their targets through the use of biological and chemical weapons, more so than nonreligious terrorist groups.[4] It is also worth noting that religious-extremist organizations, in their march to "cleanse" or refashion society, do not necessarily seek publicity and therefore may not claim responsibility for their attacks. "The religious-extremist group does not need headlines in the newspaper or the lead story on the television news," writes Post, "for its primary audience is God."[5]

In terms of structure, a religious-extremist operation often takes the form of a commander-cadre organization, with a central figure assuming a hands-on approach to its members and their illicit activities. "He trains them, provides housing and/or salaries, provides for their families in the event that they die as 'martyrs,' and, in many cases, punishes them if they disobey his orders," writes terrorism expert Jessica Stern.[6] "A commander-cadre organization is essentially a terrorist army."[7] Contrasted with other types of religious-extremist operations, commander-cadre organizations, which tend to find a home in those nations that advocate terrorism or at least turn a blind eye it, pose the greatest danger to society because they are the best-equipped, logistically and often financially, to wage large-scale assaults. In the Middle East, numerous jihadi organizations are distinguished by their commander-cadre structures and mass-casualty aspirations.

Boko Haram. The world's deadliest terrorist organization at the present time, Boko Haram, offers an example. Surpassing even ISIS in its kill rate according to the *New York Times*, Boko Haram's formal designation is *Jama'atu Ahlis Sunna Lidda'awati wal-Jihad*, meaning "People Committed to the Propagation of the Prophet's Teachings and Jihad."[8] Operating within a commander-cadre structure, the leader of this radical Islamic organization is currently Abubakar Shekau, with the rank-and-file membership numbering well into the thousands. Notwithstanding its vertical chain-of-command, Boko Haram is flexible enough to allow a handful of its cells to function more or less autonomously, an adaptability that is thought to contribute to the group's success.

As to its objectives, the organization presently seeks to impose, in large swaths of Central Africa, Sharia law: strict religious and moral regulation drawn from the Koran and from the life and teachings of the prophet Mohammed. It is an aim, moreover, that the group attempts to achieve largely through the scope of a rifle. "[P]rivate citizens are overwhelmingly targeted, most often with firearms," reads a report from the Institute for Economics and Peace, a situation that results in "very high levels of deaths per attack."[9]

In the longer term, the transnational organization's ambitions extend far beyond Nigeria, Chad, Niger, and Cameroon, the countries in which it presently carries out its missions. "Boko Haram's ultimate objective is to bring all of mankind under *sharia* governance," reports The Clarion Project, a non-profit that monitors Islamic extremism.[10] As a commander-cadre organization, then, Boko Haram demonstrates the immense danger that a tightly-structured, monocratic terrorist operation, one claiming to adhere to a fundamentalist-religious ideology, may pose to society.

At the other end of the structural spectrum are extremist networks, both "non-virtual" and "virtual," which are comprised of individuals, groups, or sub-networks. To be found not only in religious-extremist terrorism but in the non-religious varieties as well, a network is different from a commander-cadre organization by its lack of a vertical hierarchy and conventional chain of command. It may lack a leader as well, or it may have a nominal head who refrains from planning and executing terrorist attacks but rather stimulates the networks' participants to do so. "Leaders inspire operatives to take action on their own," writes Stern.[11]

In terms of the distinction between non-virtual and virtual networks, the former typically entails direct, face-to-face interaction among its members, whereas the latter may exist largely in cyberspace, where participants locate one another online and collaborate by means of coded or encrypted messages. Louis Beam, a white nationalist associated with the Ku Klux Klan and the Aryan Brotherhood, was an early proponent of such non-hierarchical, leader-free configurations. His 1983 essay, titled "Leaderless Resistance" and published in *The Seditionist*, argued that the moment had arrived in American society for extremists to move beyond traditional organizational structures.[12] Commander-cadre setups, he argued, were becoming outmoded and increasingly ineffective. In their place, he called for the creation of webs in which individual members plan and perform extremist acts on their own or in bands of two to three people, which Beam believed would make it more difficult for law enforcement to detect and defeat them. Regarding the response to his proposition, extremists embraced it at the time, with leaderless resistance gaining even greater traction among American activists in the 1990s and among foreign extremists in the twenty-first century, most notably in the Middle East.

Former CIA Operations Officer Marc Sageman has described how leaderless resistance, or virtual networks, emerged in Iraq after the 2003 U.S.-led invasion and occupation of that nation.[13] Scores of Iraqis, enraged by the destruction of their country, sought to join al-Qaeda's fight against the West but were unable to do so because the terrorist system had been forced underground. Their solution: create self-financed, virtual networks, and through them secure training in terror techniques and other crucial assistance. "They [had] no physical headquarters or sanctuary," says Sageman, "but the tolerant, virtual environment of the Internet [offered] them a semblance of unity and purpose."[14] Certainly this decentralized configuration, which he called a "leaderless jihad," should not be taken lightly.[15] "What makes leaderless resistance so potentially dangerous is the prospect of an individual or small cell obtaining a WMD [weapon of mass destruction] or employing innovative tactics in a particularly lethal manner," writes counterproliferation expert George Michael, formerly of the Air War College.[16]

Army of God. An example, one much closer to home, can be found in the Army of God (AOG), a U.S.–centered Christian extremist network that vehemently opposes abortion. In basic respects, the AOG illustrates the difference between a commander-cadre organization and a network arrangement. Equally important, it provides a contrast between an entity like Boko Haram that proclaims the grand aspiration of transforming society along fundamentalist lines and the narrower objectives of many virtual networks that attempt to change a specific practice or supposed iniquity within a given population.

It was in 1982 that the Army of God came into existence, a period when the United States was already being subjected to terrorist attacks from religious-extremist groups and movements. Of the latter, perhaps the most notorious was Christian Identity, a movement that still exists today and is averse to African Americans, Jews, gay men and lesbians, and the U.S. government. The Army of God, by comparison, focuses on those people involved in the practice of pregnancy termination.

In its formative years, the aforementioned Louis Beam was associated with the AOG network, but he did not serve as its leader nor did anyone else. An anonymously-penned Army of God manual states that God is its commander.[17] The same source explains that the network's covert activists, which it refers to as "termites" and "remnants," do not communicate with each other, just as they normally do know about one another's terrorist activities.[18] As to how its members come into the fold, often they are inspired by provocative writings on AOG's website or steered into the network by like-minded people. Subsequent to this, they conceive and carry out their own attacks in the name of the Army of God.

To facilitate would-be terrorists, the AOG manual provides instructions for arson, targeted assassinations, and bomb-making, with the latter's components ranging from butyric acid, used to make stink bombs, to more dangerous materials such as ammonium nitrate and plastic explosives. It is, to be sure, potentially deadly information and the network's members take it to heart. The Army of God has claimed responsibility for numerous attacks, starting with the 1982 kidnapping of a physician in Granite City, Illinois, and continuing through a succession of shootings and bombings at abortion clinics and women's health centers across the nation.

Between its inception and 1998, for instance, the Army of God carried out twenty-four domestic terror attacks, among them armed assaults, assassinations, and explosions at abortion clinics. In one spectacular incident, a bombing was staged at the 1996 Summer Olympics in Atlanta by AOG adherent Eric Robert Rudolph, who opposed the state of Georgia's position on abortion and hoped to force the Games' closure as a means of publicizing the issue. Killed in the nitroglycerin and dynamite-propelled blast were a Turkish man and an American woman, with another 111 people sustaining injuries.

In more recent times, the Army of God, while continuing to vigorously oppose abortion, has become increasingly anti-government in its rhetoric. Then, too, it has positioned itself against the LGBT community, despite the fact that sexual orientation is unrelated to the abortion controversy. To this end, AOG "termites" have burned gay and lesbian establishments, and, siding with their Islamic-extremist counterparts, praised the beheadings of gay men in Saudi Arabia. "Let us give thanks," said Michael Bray, an AOG minister and father of ten, referring to the barbaric custom.[19] It was Bray who was convicted of conspiracy and possession of explosives in relation to a string of bombings at abortion clinics and the offices of women's advocacy organizations on the East Coast.

The third and final form of religious-extremism that presents a threat of terrorism, including bioterrorism, centers on what social scientists refer to as "new religions."[20] Among other spiritual approaches and alternative religions, this classification encompasses new-age systems as well as certain sects or cults. Structurally, a cult is a prime example of a commander-cadre configuration in that it is an exclusive entity that revolves around the pronouncements of an authoritarian leader whom the membership may regard as tantamount to a deity. Invariably, the figure is at once compelling and controlling, and thus is in a key position to manipulate adherents' thoughts and actions. "Especially for closed religious cults, the dynamic is one of a charismatic leader who holds total sway over his followers," writes Post.[21] Not surprisingly, a principal requirement is total devotion both to the leader and to the cult's doctrines. "No doubt or doubters are permitted in these powerful hermetically sealed closed organizations."[22]

In terms of the threat of terrorism, so-called doomsday sects or cults, those uncompromising groups that embrace *apocalypticism*—the belief that the end of the world is at hand—present a particular risk. While most groups of this type are peaceful and limit their contact with society due to its supposedly corrupting influence, at least one of them, the Aum Shinrikyo sect in Japan, has adopted the opposite tack. Repeatedly, it has provoked Japanese society, seeking to hasten the so-called "end times" by triggering chaos and conflict through the use of biological and chemical weapons. Distinguished by a mélange of Buddhist and Hindu elements, this sizable organization also draws upon the prophecies of Nostradamus while embracing a handful of Christian beliefs harvested from the Book of Revelation. Since Chapter Seven focuses exclusively on Aum Shinrikyo and its bioterrorist acts, it will not be revisited at this point. Suffice it to say, the organization represents rather vividly the dangers that an extremist-religious sect may pose to a population, especially a group that has access to biological and chemical agents.

Political Extremism: Right-Wing

A second category of terrorism stems from reactionary political elements. While several varieties exist, arguably the deadliest are to be found in the more conservative or right-wing segments of society, at least in the United States. "Right-wing terrorism," says Post, "includes those groups seeking to preserve the status and privileges of a 'dominant' race or ethnicity."[23] In the U.S., such groups, which encompass self-described militias, are often vehemently pro-white, standing in staunch opposition to the African American and Hispanic communities and increasingly to the Muslim community as well. Some also exhibit anti–Semitism, insisting, for instance, that a clandestine Jewish clique has a death grip on the nation. And they may evince sexist and antigay sentiments and behaviors. Whatever their preferred target, the groups insist that the "real America" is being usurped by interlopers, deviants, renegades, or inferior races, and that this state of affairs must be reversed.

The Order. One such organization, "The Order," was a domestic neo–Nazi outfit formed in 1983 by Robert Jay Mathews. Described by attorney Morris Dees as "an Aryan Nations offshoot," it sought to trigger a revolt against the U.S. government, which the group claimed was controlled by powerful and persuasive Jews.[24] To raise funds, the group's members robbed banks and carried out "mobile thefts" using armored cars, as well as operating a counterfeiting ring. In terms of their terrorist acts, they burned synagogues and performed targeted assassinations, among other crimes. Dees notes that The Order also implemented a system that Louis Beam initially proposed, one that rewarded killings. "The system gave point values for eliminating certain types of people, from 'street niggers' to race traitors to the U.S. president," writes Dees. "The murder of a street cop was worth one-tenth of a point," he adds, "while the assassination of the president counted for a whole point, the amount needed to become an 'Aryan Warrior.'"[25]

Concerning assassinations, The Order gained notoriety in 1984 for the gangland-style murder of Alan Berg, a talk-show host at a Denver radio station. Berg's liberal, on-air comments coupled with his Jewish faith caused him to rise to the number-two spot on The Order's hit list, with the host being sprayed with bullets as he stepped out of his Volkswagen Beetle on a warm summer evening. At the ensuing trial—and to considerable public consternation—none of The Order's members who were brought before the court were convicted of homicide. Two were convicted on conspiracy, racketeering, and civil rights charges, however; federal offenses that carry stiff penalties.

More recently, right-wing terrorists have included a growing number of lone wolves, who, in many instances, become radicalized through the Internet. The 2015 mass murder at a historic African American church in Charleston, South Carolina, offers an example of a right-wing attack committed by a lone wolf. In this case, Dylann Storm Roof, a twenty-one-year-old white man, shot to death nine African American men and women during a prayer service. Holding anti-black and anti–Semitic beliefs, it was reported that Roof had previously made inflammatory, racist comments on white supremacist websites, and, even more incriminating, penned an angry manifesto in which he explained that it was essential for him to murder African Americans, that it was his calling.[26] "[S]omeone has to have the bravery to take [the fight] to the real world, and I guess that has to be me," he wrote.[27]

Of course, the fight about which right-wing terrorists speak is invariably a one-sided and bloody affair, with unsuspecting, unarmed citizens being singled out for assault. And this practice of attacking those who are defenseless places right-wing terrorists in close company with their religious-extremist brethren. But unlike certain religious-extremist groups—the Aum Shinrikyo sect comes to mind—right-wing terrorists appear to favor firearms and bombs over more sophisticated biological weapons, perhaps because the former are readily available, less complicated to devise and deploy, and well-suited to single assassinations or small-group killings. Accordingly, it is expected that groups of this type will continue using conventional weapons, especially since the spectacles that result, especially from bombings, are immediate, dramatic, and highly intimidating.

In terms of the future of right-wing terrorism in the United States, it has been on the increase in recent years and may well continue to rise. A 2014 survey conducted with the assistance of the Police Executive Research Forum, one that questioned nearly four hundred law enforcement agencies from coast to coast, found that seven percent of them considered right-wing domestic terrorists, such as anti-government extremists, to constitute a severe threat in their districts. By comparison, only three percent regarded Islamic extremists to present the same danger.[28] And these perceived menaces are backed up by statistics. Since the 2001 attacks on the World Trade Center and the Pentagon, the number of American citizens killed by homegrown, right-wing terrorists has far been greater than those who have died at the hands of Islamic extremists.[29] As terrorism experts Charles Kurzman and David Schanzer conclude from their post–9/11 research, "right-wing, anti-government extremism is the leading source of ideological violence in America."[30]

On this point, it should be noted that the United States is not alone when it comes to this form of radicalism. Far-right terrorism is alive and well in other countries, too. Between 1999 and 2011, for instance, Germany was home to the xenophobic, anti-government National Socialist Underground (NSU), a small but vicious neo–Nazi group that carried out lethal attacks against immigrants and law enforcement officers. Unfortunately, this brand of right-wing violence is not expected to diminish any time soon, particularly in Europe, where recent upsurges in asylum-seeking populations have sparked brutal nationalistic repercussions.

Political Extremism: Left-Wing

Less of a threat, at least at the present time, are left-wing terrorist organizations. These groups, according to the FBI, "generally profess a revolutionary socialist doctrine and view themselves as protectors of the people against the 'dehumanizing effects' of capitalism and imperialism."[31] Their acts of violence, which include bombings, kidnappings, and other high-profile offenses, are most often motivated by the desire to draw public attention to their cause.

In the twentieth century, the preponderance of left-wing terrorist groups thrived between the 1960s and the 1980s, especially in Western nations. Subsequent to this, their number began to fall due partly to the collapse of the Soviet Union and the ensuing decline in communism's ideological influence. That said, far-left terrorism was a formidable phenomenon during its hardiest period, one whose deeds were perhaps best exemplified by the West German social-revolutionary group Baader-Meinhof, even today the subject of academic studies, documentaries, feature films, and popular literature.

The Baader-Meinhof Gang. Although it eventually came to be known as the Red Army Faction, the organization that was originally dubbed the Baader-Meinhof Gang was in operation between 1970 and 1998. Composed of twenty-three commando units, it quickly became successful in striking fear in the West German political establishment as well as in that nation's financial sector.

Regarding its philosophical foundation, the group maintained that West Germany was being managed by former Nazis, with the nation itself being a puppet of the U.S. government.[32] For these reasons, the group was determined to bring down West Germany's capitalistic system through a campaign of terror, one that targeted bankers, prominent members of the business community, magistrates, media figures, and U.S. military personnel stationed in that country. Its methods consisted of shootings and bombings, although Baader-Meinhof members also played key roles in the 1976 skyjacking of Air France Flight 139, arguably the most spectacular terrorist attack in modern aviation history. Then there were the kidnappings.

On September 5, 1977, Baader-Meinhof launched the mission that was perhaps the most emblematic of its disdain for capitalism and for the former Nazis who had gone on to occupy powerful positions in post-war West Germany. The target: Hanns-Martin Schleyer, a one-time member of the Hitler Youth and the Nazi Party, as well as an SS officer during Hitler's reign. By the time the Baader-Meinhof Gang caught up with him in the mid–1970s, Schleyer had become a wealthy and influential industrialist, president of the Federation of German Industries, and president of the German Employers' Association. As such, he represented everything the left-wing group despised.

It was in Cologne that the abduction took place. On a late summer's day, the limousine in which Schleyer was traveling came to a stop so that a pedestrian, a woman pushing a baby carriage, could cross the street. But once the woman, a Baader-Meinhof agent, was in front of the car, she stood stock-still, immobilizing the vehicle along with the police escort that was shadowing it. With lightning speed, five masked terrorists riddled both vehicles with machine-gun fire, then dragged Schleyer into an idling getaway car. Killed in the confrontation were Schleyer's chauffeur and three police officers.

During the next few weeks, the Baader-Meinhof cell held their hostage in a Cologne high-rise, while demanding, in exchange for his freedom, the release of eleven prisoners incarcerated in Stammheim prison. Foremost among them was Andreas Baader, one of the group's founders. But, alas, it was not to be. On the night of October 17th, Baader, in his prison cell, was shot in the neck from a distance of twelve to sixteen inches, with officials classifying his death a suicide. And his was not the only one. That same evening, two other Baader-Meinhof prisoners were also reported to have killed themselves in their prison cells, one by shooting, the other by hanging. Naturally, suspicions arose at once that the government had ordered the prisoners' executions. Whatever the truth of the matter, "Death Night," as it became known, was followed by still another death the next day when the Baader Meinhof team, in retaliation, killed Hanns-Martin Schleyer himself and dumped his body in the trunk of a green Audi 1000. "Freedom through armed, anti-imperialist struggle," read a note left by a commando.[33]

Owing to more sophisticated police surveillance in conjunction with the reunification of East and West Germany in 1990, the Baader-Meinhof Gang gradually faded from sight, officially disbanding in 1998. All told, the group, in the course of its existence, killed thirty people, injured another two hundred, and intimidated thousands, thus making it one of the deadliest left-wing terrorist operations of the modern age.

Special Interest Terrorism

Still another source of terrorism, a source that does not fit neatly within the religious-extremist classification or the traditional left- or right-wing political designations, is one that addresses itself to a specific cause. Most often, animal rights or the preservation of the environment is the point of contention, particularly in Western European and North American nations. Of course, there are several organizations that oppose, in a peaceful and constructive fashion, the exploitation of animals and the mismanagement of the environment. Among such non-violent special interest groups are the Animal Defense League and People for the Ethical Treatment of Animals (PETA), as well as the Sierra Club and the environmental movement Greenpeace, which is provocative at times but not intentionally harmful toward others. The terrorist designation is applied only when an individual or group purposely sets out to inflict serious damage on people or property, with examples including such leaderless resistance networks as the Animal Liberation Front (ALF) and the Earth Liberation Front (ELF), a covert web of environmental extremists.

As to the way in which their aggression manifests, it nearly always involves property destruction, not interpersonal violence, and in this sense is distinct from many religious-extremist, right-wing, and left-wing terrorist groups. By damaging public or private property, special interest groups and networks hope to draw attention to an issue, prevent the continuation of a controversial practice, or intimidate or punish a target.

In terms of their methods, when a group's concern is the environment, the term "eco-terrorism" may be used to describe its aggressive deeds. For instance, a non-terrorist organization that opposes commercial tree removal in California's redwood forests may block the roads used by a timber harvesting company so as to impede its operations. No physical harm is done to people or property, since the desired effect is disruption only. A eco-terrorist group, on the other hand, may engage in "monkeywrenching," sabotaging the companies' operations on a truly dangerous scale. For instance, eco-terrorists have driven nails and iron spikes into trees, thereby potentially destroying workers' equipment when they attempt to fell them with industrial saws. And while perpetrators have, in some cases, spray-painted the letter "S" onto the bark of sabotaged trees to warn workers away from them, most often the trees have gone unmarked.

In the most infamous episode of tree spiking, a newly-married, twenty-three-year-old mill worker in California, George Alexander, was nearly decapitated when a band saw he was operating tore into an eleven-inch nail. "The blade ripped through Alexander's safety helmet and face shield, tore his left cheek, cut through his jawbone, knocked out upper and lower teeth and nearly severed his jugular vein," writes the *Los Angeles Times*.[34] "I'm only here because my friend Rick Phillips held my veins together in the hour before the ambulance came," Alexander later said.[35] Although the victim, who was also struck in the head with a section of the tree, required plastic surgery and dentures, environmental activist David Foreman conveyed his regret about what he considered the principal victim, the ecosystem itself. "I think it's unfortunate that somebody got hurt, but you know I quite honestly am more concerned about old-growth forests, spotted owls, and wolverines and salmon—and nobody is forcing people to cut those trees."[36] Foreman is a founder of the organization *Earth First!* and the publisher of a how-to book about tree-spiking and other "eco-defense" measures.[37] Decentralized in structure, *Earth First!* has been classified as a terrorist organization by the Mountain States Legal Foundation.[38]

More than with other types of terrorist entities, biodefense experts worry that special-interest extremists might come to favor biological or chemical agents in their assaults. Unfortunately, there is a precedent for their use of microbial pathogens and biological toxins. An animal rights entity in Britain was alleged in 1989 to have tainted grocery store products to oppose what it regarded as the commercial exploitation of animals. In the course of this program of economic sabotage, members purportedly injected supermarket turkeys with mercury so that customers would be fearful of purchasing them. They also tainted eggs, then sketched onto them a skull and crossbones to alert buyers to the risk. And in still another action, British animal rights extremists claimed to have laced Mars candy bars with rat poison. "No poison was found," writes Stern, "but Mars reported losses of $4.5 million."[39]

A similar concern—the deliberate deployment of pathogens and toxins—also applies to radical environmentalists. "Ecoterrorists would be attracted to biological weapons," writes former UN bioweapons inspector Rocco Casagrande, "because of the irony of using nature to reverse the depredations of mankind."[40] Casagrande points out that such agents additionally hold the capacity to inflict severe economic damage. "Biological agents could allow ecoterrorists to devastate genetically engineered crops, remove livestock from pristine grassland, or economically ruin a fertilizer manufacturer."[41]

In these types of attack, eco-terrorists would not target healthy crops; only genetically modified plants would be affected. Likewise, animals would not be harmed but rather "liberated" so that they might graze in less exceptional areas. Yet there does exist another terrorist element that intentionally sets out to inflict damage on the environment, and it is composed of radical political factions. Whereas environmental terrorists claim to be motivated by the desire to protect nature and ensure its preservation, extremists of other stripes turn to ecoterrorism as a means of exacting a cost from their enemies by spoiling the land and air. "Causing harmful environmental changes and this way terrorizing people, is the main goal of this type of terrorism," writes Polish terrorism expert Mirosława Skawińska.[42]

> Ecoterrorists often target natural oil producing installations. Petroleum leaking from damaged pipelines, refinery plants, petroleum mining shafts or oil carrying tankers contaminate soils, waters, [and] cause fires, which in turn cause air pollution. Countries which are listed as eco terrorists are: Kuwait, Israel, Iran, Iraq or Lebanon.[43]

Skawińska foresees the future of eco-terrorism as leaning increasingly toward the use of bioweapons, noting that, among counterterrorism experts, a "biological attack is considered to be more probable than a nuclear one, and also more deadly than a chemical attack."[44]

Unfortunately, there is also the prospect of accidents and aftereffects. A terrorist group, regardless of its type, may have no intention of visiting harm upon the ecosystem yet its attacks may result in environmental injury all the same. For instance, an offensive launched in 1981 by an Irish paramilitary organization, an action designed to cause economic harm, secondarily produced significant biological damage in the form of air and water pollution. In this case, the nature of the group was not eco-terrorist but rather nationalistic, the final category of violent extremism to be examined in this chapter.

Nationalist and Separatist Terrorism

In contrast to the aims of the religious-extremist, left- and right-wing, and special interest categories of terrorism, nationalist and ethno-nationalist groups view themselves as being engaged in a fight against subordination, as waging a war for independence and self-determination. Like them, separatist groups also seek self-determination and may further pursue the establishment of a sovereign, breakaway state.

A second distinction has to do with the groups' visibility and social integration. Whereas the members of a religious-extremist cult or a left-wing social-revolutionary group like the Baader-Meinhof Gang tend to sequester themselves from society, emerging only to perpetrate attacks and then return to the underground, the members of nationalist, ethno-nationalist, or separatist groups may be well-known in their communities. For that matter, their communities may tacitly support the extremists' illicit activities, as was the case for the Irish group mentioned earlier, the Provisional Irish Republican Army, the guerrilla element of the IRA which was most active between 1969 and 1997.

Provisional Irish Republican Army. Like the nationalist Palestinian Liberation Organization (PLO) in the Occupied Territories and the separatist Basque ETA in Spain and southwestern France, the IRA's goal was wholly political: it sought to bring to an end British rule in Northern Ireland. A unified Ireland under Irish governance was its desire. Accordingly, its targets were situated in Northern Ireland and England, although the organization occasionally carried out acts of aggression elsewhere in Europe.

In terms of the IRA's techniques, assassinations and bombings were its favored methods and included the use of car bombs as well as incendiary devices planted on buses and trains. Besides public transportation, its targets encompassed basic components of Britain's infrastructure, along with mundane entities such as telephone booths and airport parking lots. To shock the public and disrupt the tourist industry, the IRA also detonated bombs in crowded tourist venues like the Tower of London. Regarding the attacks mentioned earlier, the ones that damaged the ecosystem, they occurred in 1981 near Moville, a small port city in Northern Ireland.

Over a two-day period at the height of winter, the IRA carried out four offensives, one of them directed at a British ship delivering coal from Liverpool, England to Coleraine, Northern Ireland. Christened the *Nellie M,* the eleven hundred-ton ship was anchored on Lough Foyle, a bay in the northernmost region of Northern Ireland. In this covert operation aimed at wreaking economic havoc, seven masked IRA gunmen stormed onto the *Nellie M*, took control of the vessel, and planted bombs below deck. As the terrorists were escaping, multiple explosions rocked the ship and sent it to the bottom of Lough Foyle. "At high tide," reads an account in the *Chicago Tribune*, "only the superstructure [main deck assembly] of the Nellie M was visible above the waters."[45] Unfortunately, the bombing not only destroyed the ship and its cargo, but it also caused considerable environmental harm, with coal dust filling the air as well as contaminating Lough Foyle and a portion of the North Atlantic to which it connects.[46]

In 1977, the IRA's paramilitary operations came to an end when the organization agreed to a ceasefire. A key element of the pact stipulated that the IRA's political arm, Sinn Fein, be permitted to participate in the Northern Ireland peace talks. In all, the IRA, in the course of its twenty-eight years of paramilitary engagement, murdered nearly four thousand people and injured tens of thousands of civilians.[47]

With the exception of its reckless actions on Lough Foyle, the IRA seems to have refrained from deliberately harming the environment in its scores of attacks over the years, and the organization is not known to have ever used biological weapons. Perhaps this can be partly attributed to the difficulty involved in developing and deploying them. Certainly this has been the case for many other terrorist groups, whether self-sufficient or state-sponsored. With increasing global access to the knowledge and materials needed to assemble a biological weapon, however, this state of play may soon change. And this brings us to an examination of the factors that may encourage or discourage future terrorist organizations and networks from pursuing a biological weapons agenda.

The Bioterror Calculation: Incentives and Disincentives

When assessing the prospects of a terrorist group adopting pathogens or toxins as weapons, it is important to take into account the societal taboo that, for centuries, has helped suppress this method of violence. Weighed against other types of aggression, biological attacks have long been regarded as among the most reprehensible owing to their stealthy, underhanded nature coupled with their potential to wipe out large swaths of the population through an uncontrolled contagion. Regrettably, it was a taboo the Aum Shinrikyo group breached in the 1990s when it dispersed anthrax in a public setting, with the sect also releasing sarin gas, a nerve agent, and the neurotoxin botulinum. With these calculated acts against humanity, the doomsday sect opened the door, at least theoretically, to biological and chemical assaults by other extremist outfits.[48] But not only did the Aum Shinrikyo organization set a precedent by releasing pathogens and toxins in public venues; its actions also demonstrated that the organization could endure after defying this long-standing, transcultural prohibition. Accordingly, the lesson for extremist groups was a heartening one: it is possible for an organization to use bioweapons against civilians without the assault spelling the end of the organization itself. That said, there remain powerful drawbacks to resorting to such treacherous tactics.

Especially in the Middle East, a region in which terrorist groups have been known to enjoy the backing of local populations and sometimes that of states themselves, the use of biological agents may threaten to undermine such accommodating circumstances. "An attack introduces risk for the terrorist because [of] the potential for a loss of support from their constituents," says Daniel Gerstein, a strategist and policy expert.[49] Given that bio-attacks are universally rejected as an atrocious form of warfare, regional advocates of a terrorist group that decides to carry out this type of assault may thereafter shun the organization, just as a supportive state may sever its ties to an extremist entity whose actions violate the Biological Weapons Convention, an international agreement to which the state itself may be a signatory. While a terrorist group may remain intact after dispersing a biological agent, then, it may forfeit essential sources of support.

It is also worth mentioning that a terrorist organization's long-term goals may be instrumental when contemplating the use of microbial agents as instruments of aggression. Whereas an apocalyptic religious sect hoping to usher in the "end times" may have little worry about the backlash it will suffer when unleashing a lethal microorganism, a politically-oriented or special interest group may be greatly concerned about the negative repercussions that will likely ensue. And understandably so. If an extremist entity hopes to eventually take part in a country's decision-making processes, as did the Provisional IRA, employing biological weapons against unwary citizens will almost certainly guarantee that the group will never be afforded a "place at the table." A heinous act of this magnitude would negate any future overtures the group might make toward inclusion in society. This imperviousness to the social and political consequences is one reason counterterrorism experts contend that a religious-extremist entity would be more inclined to use a bioweapon than the typical political-extremist or special interest organization.

Still another aspect of the decision to release pathogenic agents has to do with the advanced skills that are required to fashion a feasible bioweapon, with experts holding conflicting opinions as to the degree to which contemporary extremist groups may have access to such expertise. Gerstein explains that there are two divergent camps, "one that says the necessary steps are too difficult for the terrorist to accomplish and one that says that bioterror is imminent."[50] Of the two, the prevailing opinion is that devising and deploying a bioweapon remains a very tricky feat, which presumably is why a sweeping biological attack has yet to take place on American soil.

As Gerstein points out in his book *Bioterror in the 21st Century*, the nation of Iraq, despite intensive efforts in the 1980s, failed to weaponize the anthrax bacterium.[51] And this was a wealthy, Middle Eastern country with a formidable WMD program, one that boasted an abundance of top-notch research scientists. It is even less likely that a band of terrorists would succeed in weaponizing a pathogen, especially in the absence of substantial state sponsorship.

In addition, there is the problem of time. Due to the numerous steps involved in crafting a biological weapon, from researching the process to acquiring and priming a suitable pathogen to assembling an effective deployment apparatus, a terrorist group would run the risk of discovery by the authorities. As is the case with any type of WMD, the longer the research, development, and implementation phases of the operation, the greater the chances of a security breach. So while a well-funded terrorist outfit might be able to conduct a protracted biowarfare program, it would risk being detected and neutralized long before a weapon could be finalized. At least this is an argument put forth by those who maintain that a bio-attack is far from imminent.

Those taking the opposite position, on the other hand, insist that it is only a matter of time before a terrorist organization launches a biological assault; that the task of creating a bioweapon, while challenging, is not necessarily a prolonged one, not anymore. Returning to our Iraq example, whereas the Middle Eastern nation was unable to weaponize anthrax in the 1980s, it might well be within the same research team's capabilities today. And this applies to terrorists as well. "Some analysts consider that terrorists could develop [biological] weapons very quickly once they set their minds to it," says Gerstein.[52] It is a state of affairs that stems, in large measure, from increased globalization and profound advances in biotechnology.

The fact is, the fields of industrial biology and biotechnology have made tremendous leaps in recent years, just as globalization, during the same period, has increased dramatically owing to a flurry of developments, among them enhanced digital communication and the growth of the Internet. As well, the open-sourcing of information, especially that which is contained in academic journals, has made crucial material accessible to virtually anyone who seeks it. And this includes groundbreaking discoveries and innovations in biological and genetic research, a potential goldmine of facts and figures for those hoping to devise a biological weapon.

"Academic journals contain much of the information [terrorists] require, and an exhaustive literature search through sources such as *Acta Scandinavia* and the Merck Index can provide the information that they need," write defense consultants Nadine Gurr and Benjamin Cole.[53] The pair adds that the Aum Shinrikyo sect, whose operations were based at a remote location near Mount Fuji, began in precisely this manner, with a comprehensive review of the research literature together with a massive download of biological and chemical information mined from the databases of the Brookhaven National Laboratory in Upton, Long Island (New York).[54]

Predictably, biodefense experts have been quite vocal in expressing concern about the role academic journals and related resources may play in bioterrorist activities. Some have also conveyed their dismay about the Human Genome Project, specifically its overseers' decision to make available to the public fundamental genetic information. They fear that terrorists or rogue states may, in due course, exploit this material; for instance, by altering the genetic code of a virus so as to render it more resilient and infectious. A distressing development, it would depend on the group's ability to acquire the know-how to manipulate human DNA.

At first blush, obtaining the expertise to devise a biological weapon, especially one that would involve genetic engineering, might seem to be an insurmountable task. Yet to succeed at this undertaking, a terrorist group would have only to recruit a team of individuals with proficiencies in the requisite areas; it would not need to furnish its entire membership with crash courses in microbiology and biotechnology. And today, it is surprisingly easy to track down scientists having the skills to build a bioweapon, even one entailing genetic engineering.

"What was once considered to be esoteric knowledge about how to culture and disperse infectious agents has now spread amongst tens of thousands of people," write Gurr and Cole.[55] Of course, the overwhelming majority of scientists are, and will remain, thoroughly ethical in their actions, but there does exist that tiny fraction that is willing to work for a fee, motivated either by political or religious ideology or by financial need. The former USSR, Gurr and Cole point out, is illustrative. "[F]ollowing the dissolution of the Soviet Union, large numbers of engineers who had previously worked on developing WMD were made unemployed or simply not paid by the government the successor states," they write. "Some of these engineers have allegedly become available for hire."[56]

The financial costs of a biological warfare program may also enter the equation. Of the three types of WMDs—biological, chemical, and nuclear—biological weapons are the least expensive to devise. In fact, many of the pathogens that terrorists might seek exist freely in nature and may also be found in laboratories throughout the world. And not only are they inexpensive and, with the right connections, attainable; a tiny amount of pathogenic material may be sufficient to produce extensive damage, particularly if a bio-attack leads to a contagion. By comparison, a chemical or nuclear assault impacts only those with whom the principal agent makes contact. That is to say, chemical and nuclear agents are not transmissible.

Readily available, too, is much of the equipment required to fashion a bioweapon. For several years now, experts have maintained that a terrorist cell could concoct a bio-weapon using materials purchased on the Internet or from a home improvement store. From used laboratory equipment posted for sale online—apparatuses that duplicate DNA, for instance—to "home fermenters" stocked by chain stores across the United States, assembling a BW workshop is today both viable and affordable, with how-to instruction manuals for constructing bioweapons available on the Internet.

Based on the preceding litany of advantages that terrorists currently enjoy, it would appear that an ambitious extremist operation could, with relatively little difficulty, devise and deploy a formidable biological weapon. Scientists and technicians are available for hire, pathogens are accessible, equipment is easily obtainable, and instructions are present online for the downloading. Given these developments, then, the question is why society has not already endured a succession of bio-attacks in recent years. And the answer may stem, in large measure, from fear on the part of terrorist organizations; a sobering recognition of the perils inherent in managing a bioweapons program.

"There are safety hazards for individuals working [with] these pathogens," write Gurr and Cole, who point out that "specialized state-run facilities have rigorous safety mechanisms and procedures to protect staff."[57] In the case of a terrorist group, financial constraints, time limitations, and other factors may prevent it from fully adhering to the same stringent standards required of a professional laboratory, one whose compliance is ensured through external oversight. For this reason, a terrorist group's BW project may pose a danger to the group itself, with this presumably being an overarching reason for extremists' reluctance to embark on such a program. Those creating a bio-weapon, along with other members of the organization, could find themselves its first victims, casualties of their own deadly microorganism.

Yet there is a persuasive counterpoint. Some experts argue that seasoned biological researchers and technicians would be smart enough to contain the hazards to which they might be exposed. Experienced microbiologists would know that cutting corners could cost them their lives when dealing with lethal microbes. That said, Gurr and Cole have called attention to the Aum Shinrikyo sect, whose in-house scientists, despite being well-versed in safety procedures, not only exposed themselves and others to the bacterium that produces Q fever, but then failed to follow proper decontamination procedures.[58]

Still another reason society has not suffered a greater number of bioterror attacks is believed to be due to the complexity involved in building an effective dispersal mechanism, an intricate task combining microbiology and engineering. As it stands, a bioweapon is useless unless it is paired with a viable dissemination apparatus, and this can be a very difficult task when it comes to microbial dispersal. It is because obstacles in distribution may have forestalled expansive bio-attacks in the past that a future terrorist group may decide to content itself with a scaled-down offensive or with multiple, minor bio-attacks.

"Lack of an effective dispersal mechanism will force terrorists to use any [biological] agents that they manage to develop as contaminants," says Gurr and Cole.[59] As opposed to a large-scale, "open air" attack, a terrorist cell, in a more modest and constrained operation, might place a contaminant in the air-conditioning system of a building or, alternatively, in its water supply. While illness and possibly death would ensue, the assault would be far less catastrophic than one using a method capable of disseminating a pathogen in a more expansive, generalized fashion. Of course, this does not mean that more efficient methods of diffusion will not be invented in the fullness of time, and that they will find their way into the hands of terrorists. "Technologically sophisticated groups," say Gurr and Cole, "could prove capable of developing, or acquiring, efficient dispersal methods."[60] To a terrorist group hoping to intimidate its foes and wishing to attract media attention, though, a comparatively small attack in which pathogens or toxins are used as contaminants might be regarded as a resounding success. "It is possible to conceive of an outcome from a bioterror attack that results in few casualties, yet gains significant media coverage, resulting in increased visibility for the terrorist's stated goals and objectives," says Gerstein.[61]

The Tylenol poisonings of 1982, although they involved a chemical rather than a biological agent, offer an example. In this infamous episode in which the popular painkiller was laced with potassium cyanide, the result was a relatively small number of deaths, seven, in the Chicago area. All the same, it triggered a national panic, prompted the recall of thirty-one million bottles of Tylenol, and led to permanent changes in the packaging of over-the-counter medications. Financially, the incident proved to be a nightmare for the painkiller's manufacturer, Johnson & Johnson, which not only lost millions of dollars in sales, but also found it necessary to invest $100,000,000 to restore its medications' security and salvage the company's reputation.[62] It is not a stretch, then, to suggest that a small bio-attack could produce profoundly negative effects, more than sufficient to gratify a terrorist. Then, too, it should be noted that it does not require a lone-wolf terrorist or an organized terrorist operation to plan and execute a biological assault; an individual with a personal vendetta or other agenda can do it as well.

Biocrimes

"A person who is smart, determined, trained in basic microbiological techniques, and willing to take a few short-cuts on safety and go at a few technical problems in mildly unconventional ways, could conceivably do some horrible things," says Kyle Olson, a bioweapons analyst in Arlington, Virginia.[63] This is precisely the type of person who worries not only terrorism experts, but ordinary law enforcement officials as well, since they too may find themselves confronting men and women in their own localities who seek to commit biological offenses. It will be instructive, then, to distinguish between a bioterror attack, which is itself a crime, and what is referred to in law enforcement circles as a "biocrime."

According to physician-scientist Steven Schutzer and his colleagues Bruce Budowie and Ronald Atlas, "[a] biocrime is similar to an assault crime, except, instead of a gun or knife, the weapon is a pathogen or a toxin."[64] In the typical case, the perpetrator—usually there is only one—targets someone with whom he or she is familiar, from a spouse to a co-worker, and seeks to sicken or kill the person with a biological agent. By comparison, a bioterror attack typically involves a group of extremists going after a large number of people, most often civilians whose individual identities are unknown to the extremists themselves. Characteristically, a bioterror attack is far deadlier than a biocrime in terms of the number of casualties, as well as being considerably more indiscriminate in its targeting.

The motives are also different. The intentions that underlie biocrimes are the same as those found in other forms of assault, running the gamut from jealousy to retaliation to financial gain. A perpetrator may seek to exact revenge on a former lover or a business competitor, for instance, or may hope to benefit from the victim's life insurance benefits if death occurs. Seldom does a perpetrator's motive arise from a religious or political ideology, which is most often the case with bioterrorism.

As for legal consequences, biocrimes are typically addressed in the same manner as other types of criminal assault, such as shootings and beatings: locally and in conventional legal fashion. Bioterror attacks are treated differently. "In the US," write Schutzer and his colleagues, "acts of bioterrorism are federal crimes that are governed by different responses by law enforcement and public health agencies."[65]

At this point, it should be mentioned that hoaxes are far more common than those offenses that make actual use of pathogens or toxins. "The numerous hoaxes that are biocrimes include white powders found in letters that proclaim the presence of anthrax, and threatening notes claiming ricin contamination of baby food," writes the Schutzer team, referring to current trends in threats.[66]

As could be expected, a claim of anthrax, ricin, or other biological agent may be remarkably effective in alarming the victim and necessitating an emergency medical assessment and subsequent monitoring. In so doing, it presumably fulfills the perpetrator's intentions. Furthermore, such a ruse can be implemented rather easily on a larger scale, and very cheaply. This was the case in the nation's first major anthrax hoax, which occurred in 1997 when a shattered petri dish that had been holding a white substance was mailed to B'nai B'rith headquarters in Washington, D.C. An intriguing suspect who claimed to be innocent: a biodefense expert with a background in counterintelligence, a man whom the *New York Times* referred to as "Mr. Z" and who was in the city to attend a bioterrorism conference. Feeling that important biodefense issues were not being addressed, he was reportedly displeased that he had been omitted from the assembly's roster of speakers. Then the anthrax scare occurred. "The next day," reports Nicholas Kristof, "Mr. Z sent a letter to the [conference] organizer saying that he was 'rather concerned' at the omission and added: 'As was evidenced in downtown Washington, D.C. ... this topic is vital to the security of the United States."[67] Mr. Z added that he was eager to become more involved in the discussion. It is conceivable, then, that the ruse was designed to win a position on the conference's list of speakers.

Regarding the city's response to the hoax, more than a hundred B'nai B'rith employees were sequestered as a precaution, some were subjected to preventive, on-site decontamination, and seventeen others were hospitalized for observation. "[T]he hoax cost more than $2 million to handle, closed a major thoroughfare less than a mile from the White House for 10 hours, disrupted normal activities in the city and spread fear among its citizens," writes Ronald Bailey.[68] To those who carry out such deceptions, part of the appeal may be that the deed achieves its objectives without the hoaxer having to face the risk or expend the labor necessary to obtain and deploy a dangerous toxin or microorganism.

"The most critical step in ... biocrime incidents," reads a UN document on the subject, "is the acquisition of biological agents or toxins."[69] To be sure, acquisition is a challenge for the average person who lacks access to a medical or research laboratory, and it is presumably for this reason that those who hold jobs in such settings—that is, positions that offer admittance to stocks of microbes and toxins—are vastly over-represented in the commission of biocrimes.

In the United States between 2002 and the present, the agents used in biocriminal incidents have been "mostly pathogenic micro-organisms available to the perpetrator through their profession and/or study," reports the aforementioned UN study.[70] This being the case, it should come as no surprise that healthcare professionals, along with researchers in medically-oriented fields, comprise, by far, the largest category of perpetrators. Accordingly, they are the focus of the biocriminal case studies contained in Part Two of this book, together with comprehensive accounts of precedential bioterrorist operations in Japan and the United States.

◆ 3 ◆

Biohacking
Citizen Science and Societal Risk

Bioterrorism, as the previous chapter revealed, poses a threat to the population in the same way that small-scale biocriminal acts present a danger to specific individuals or clusters of individuals. Yet there is a third type of activity that some fear may culminate in biological violence as well, one comprised of "citizen scientists." Ranging from rank amateurs to professionals in various fields, these are people who undertake biological projects outside the walls of traditional institutional settings and thus far without regulation or oversight. Quite often, their experiments, which are characteristically benign, involve the manipulation of DNA, and are increasing in number and sophistication as biotechnology equipment becomes more affordable. As for their motives, biohackers conduct such experiments mainly to quench their curiosity, although some yearn to see their results acknowledged by the scientific establishment while others hope to market their findings and innovations.

"These hobbyists represent a growing strain of geekdom known as biohacking, in which do-it-yourselfers tinker with the building blocks of life in the comfort of their own homes," writes Jeanne Whalen in the *Wall Street Journal*.[1] Given the fanciful nature of the topic, it should come as no surprise that alarming stories about biohacking, always speculative, have appeared in the media in recent years, overwrought tales warning that it is all but inevitable that a daft or devious hobbyist will someday cook up a dangerous, artificial life form in a makeshift suburban lab. Of course, such over-the-top reports may be driven less by the desire to alert society to an impending danger and more by the determination to sell newspapers or serve as clickbait. Even so, it does not alter the fact that genuine perils may indeed be associated with biohacking, and that they may intensify in the coming years as hands-on biologists acquire greater expertise and more advanced equipment.

The fact is, those experimenting with DNA, from hobbyists with limited education to professional engineers and information technologists, often lack training in biosafety measures.[2] In some cases, they also lack a sufficient education in biology itself, most of all genetics, and thus may not be fully aware of the potential hazards that are present in their pursuits. It is a state of affairs that constitutes a vulnerability in the biohacking movement. Says scientist Markus Schmidt of the Biosafety Working Group, a project of the Organisation for International Dialogue and Conflict Management in Vienna, Austria:

> [T]his ultimate domestication of biology could easily lead to unprecedented safety challenges that need to be addressed: more and more people outside the traditional biotechnology community will create self-replicating machines [life] for civil and defence applications; "biohackers" will engineer new life forms at their kitchen table; and illicit substances will be produced synthetically and much cheaper.[3]

Zeroing in on biohacking in particular, he adds, "An unrestricted biohacker scenario could put the health of a biohacker, the community around him or her and the environment under unprecedented risk."[4]

It should be noted that Schmidt's apprehension centers on the well-meaning practitioner whose experiments go awry. Of even greater concern is the "garage biologist" who harbors darker motives, the man or woman who deliberately sets out to inflict harm on society. Certainly the prospect of such a person is a cause for concern, especially given the history of the traditional computer hacker. Just as there has long existed within the community of computer enthusiasts a rogue element that is bent on clandestinely spreading viruses and other malicious software, so it is reasonable to expect the eventual emergence of a breed of biohacker that strives to harm others in much the same way, but through the use of microbes, either naturally-occurring or artificially engineered.

To better understand the biohacking movement and assess the extent of the threat it poses to society, it will be useful to revisit the more conventional practice of computer hacking and the path by which biology came to be associated with it.

The Genesis of Computer Hacking

Although today we associate hacking with those shadowy figures who infect our computers with an ever-changing array of malware or who slip past firewalls and make off with our personal information, the term carried a very different meaning when it originally came into use nearly sixty years ago. This was during the early days of research and development in the field of computer technology, an inventive, invigorating, and comparatively innocent period. It is one that Gisle Hannemyr, author and lecturer at the Institute of Informatics, University of Oslo, recounted in his compelling article about the hacking phenomenon.[5]

"In the 1950s, people working with computers had much in common with artists, artisans and craftsmen," Hannemyr writes. "Skilled programmers, like all good craftsmen, had intimate knowledge and understanding of the systems they worked with."[6] An era of freedom and openness, computer aficionados ground away side by side, bouncing ideas off one another in a communal effort to advance the field. They did so, moreover, with little or no interest in financial compensation. But these halcyon days of collective creation proved to be short-lived. As the 1950s gave way to the 1960s, corporate leadership set about instituting control over this uniquely creative element of its operations, and it did so by adopting a management style in which employees were pressed into discrete areas of specialization.

"Computer workers found themselves stratified into a strict hierarchy where a 'system analyst' was to head a software development team consisting [of], in decreasing order of status and seniority, 'programmers,' 'coders,' 'testers' and 'maintainers,'" writes Hannemyr.[7] It was a pecking order that often carried over into the workspace as well, with staffers finding themselves sequestered from their colleagues. "Putting the different grade of workers in different locations further enforced the division of labor," says Hannemyr.[8] But while this management strategy was effective in bringing employees to heel and rendering their work products more quantifiable, it stifled the remarkable creativity, not to mention the *esprit de corps*, that heretofore had distinguished the same workers.

In his definitive work on the computer industry's individualists, *Hackers: Heroes of the Computer Revolution*, former *Newsweek* senior editor Steven Levy singles out one corporation that became particularly notorious for its regimentation in the 1950s: IBM, or International Business Machines.[9] "You could wander into the Computation Center … and see the stifling orderliness, down to the roped-off areas beyond which unauthorized people could not venture," he writes.[10] The buttoned-down IBM was, in Levy's words, "an empire unto itself, secretive and smug."[11] Not surprisingly, such organizations with their constraining milieus demoralized and alienated many of their more inspired employees, some of whom responded with their feet. Bright, motivated, and self-reliant, these young mavericks sought out those remaining enclaves, quite often in academic settings, where their devotion to understanding computer operations, experimentation with novel concepts, and sharing of ideas and information would still be respected and encouraged. Here, they bonded with like-minded individuals to create cohesive, innovative communities.

Three universities that became well-known for offering hands-on opportunities to such computer virtuosos were Stanford University, Massachusetts Institute of Technology (MIT), and Carnegie-Mellon University. Although computer science departments were not yet commonplace in the early 1960s, prosperous and progressive universities, like the above-mentioned institutions, did establish computer centers where determined students could, by hook or crook, gain access to state-of-the-art technology.

For the most part, these were young men, many of them electrical engineering majors, who were intrigued by the possibilities offered by the era's computers. Skipping classes and sleeping during the day, they spent their nights at their schools' twenty-four-hour computer centers writing and implementing programs, then reporting the outcomes to their comrades the next day. At MIT, a close-knit group of students with expertise in computer science adopted the term "hacking" to describe their activities, a term dating back to the college's longstanding tradition of springing pranks on the unsuspecting. These students, however, assigned the term a new meaning. To them, hacking did not involve malicious activity; it was not an arch pursuit. Rather, it was a form of creative engagement that was at once positive and productive, one that involved informed experimentation with the new technology, the aim being to advance it. "[T]o qualify as a hack," writes Levy, a pursuit had to be "imbued with innovation, style, and technical virtuosity."[12] In its purest form, hacking was an undertaking that commanded great respect within the computer community, with its participants regarded as artisans whose accomplishments were acts of brilliance and beauty.

Among the hackers' early efforts were programs that instructed computers to play music or, alternatively, translate text from various written languages. Especially noteworthy was the invention, in 1962, of one of the first digital computer video games, *Spacewar!*, a sterling achievement for the MIT group. In keeping with the group's principles and code of conduct—the "hacker ethic," as it became known—*Spacewar!* was not created for profit. In fact, the twenty-five-year-old who devised the program, Steve Russell, made not a cent from it. Instead, the project was intended to advance the field of knowledge, and thus, from the get-go, was freely available and "hackable"— that is, open to being modified and improved upon by others. "Like any other program, it was placed in the drawer for anyone to access, look at, and rewrite as they saw fit."[13] By all accounts, these pioneering hackers were a smart, idealistic, and generous lot.

In terms of the specific components of the hacker ethic, its key elements consisted of the following:

- Information is inherently free.
- Knowledge should be shared, not copyrighted, patented, licensed, or otherwise "owned" and controlled.
- The citizenry should have free and unfettered access to computer technology.

- Hands-on learning is superior to less direct forms of learning.
- A decentralized approach is superior to a centralized, bureaucratic one.
- Hacking should strive to improve the world.
- Hackers' creations can be objects of beauty and artistry.
- Hackers should be evaluated solely on the quality of their work. Educational degrees, job titles, etc., should not be a part of the appraisal.
- Autonomy is essential. Question authority.[14]

Expanding on these principles, Finnish philosopher Pekka Himanen adds that many hackers hoped to actualize themselves through their work; that they used it, in part, to reach their potential.[15] In the same vein, they were determined to disseminate their work so that humanity, as a whole, would likewise be enhanced.

As it happened, the tone of the hacker ethic shifted over the years, and it did do so partly in response to the times. Although its original components remained firmly in place into the 1970s, it was during this decade that emphasis came to be placed on those aspects that centered on freedom and autonomy. Insisting more fervently than ever that information should be freely accessible, hackers set out to secure the digital frontier for the citizenry. In this way, the computer artisans of the 1960s became the progressive activists of the 1970s, especially after the advent of the microprocessor. This proficient circle of prodigies, for instance, played an important role in expanding citizen access to computer technology by envisioning and championing public computer terminals. Even more radically, it was from within their ranks that the personal computer was born. It should come as no surprise, then, that many of these hacker-activists, from the world-class "tinkerers" to the visionaries, came to be counted among the earliest denizens of Silicon Valley.

Of course, not every computer enthusiast of the 1970s endorsed all components of the hacker ethic. Bill Gates, for one, while instrumental in bringing affordable computers to middle-class homes, railed against the notion that information is inherently free. In 1976, the twenty-year-old cofounder of Microsoft, today among the richest entrepreneurs in the world, published an open letter explaining to computer hobbyists that it was imperative that they purchase, not share, his company's software because the revenue was needed to cover the cost of continued software development.[16] Sharing such products, Gates argued, was tantamount to stealing them, and was a practice that deprived software developers of their livelihoods even as it stifled progress. "Who can afford to do professional work for nothing?" he asked.[17] But Gates' missive was met with disdain by those hobbyists who had been sharing Microsoft products, one consequence being that a number of indignant hackers set about designing their own software which they either gave away or sold at bargain-basement prices. To be sure, hacking—in this case, creating software for community use—was still alive and well.

It would be in the 1980s that the term would take on an altogether different meaning, a negative one in that it would be applied to activities that were malicious, even criminal. Hacking would now become synonymous with hostile deeds, as in illicitly entering computers, vandalizing them ("digital defacement"), hijacking and remote-controlling them, and stealing private information. And this new definition would endure. Today, "hacking" continues to be the most common expression for such destructive acts, with the term's more noble beginnings having long been forgotten. But not by everyone. In one area of pursuit, its original meaning lives on, as do many features of the hacker ethic itself; an area that involves the melding of 1960s and 1970s-style computer hacking with the biological sciences.

Biohacking

"Some people … call themselves *biohackers* and refer explicitly to the hacker movement and history," writes Alessandro Delfanti, Assistant Professor of Culture and New Media at the University of Toronto.[18] "[T]hese biohackers represent all the complexity and heterogeneity of hacker politics, and translate it into the world of biology."[19] Yet certain precepts of biohacking, also known as "wetware hacking" and "do-it-yourself biology," are more sweeping than those of their predecessors. For instance, a principal tenet of biohacking is that the citizenry not only should enjoy unrestricted access to information emerging from the life sciences, but that biological experimentation itself should be "democratized," to use the proponents' term.

"The kind of open science they foster," says Delfanti, "is one in which openness is not limited to open information sharing, but rather expresses a radical request for opening science's boundaries which allows entry for people who do not belong to its institutions."[20] Specifically, biohackers argue that anyone, even the person who lacks training in biology, should be able to freely conduct research in the life sciences and in alternative settings. The underlying philosophy: scientific engagement, like knowledge itself, belongs to the people; it is not the exclusive province of a scholarly elite ensconced in an ivory tower or a corporate research center.

Of course, this position may be considered reasonable or unreasonable depending on the particular activity. Most people would probably regard it as a sensible stance when applied to a neighborhood learning lab where inquisitive citizens gather to perform innocuous experiments. Such community facilities do exist, and they serve a useful function in fulfilling the public's interest in biology and biotechnology. Although their explorations may be more advanced, these citizen scientists are not unlike those adolescents in previous decades who carried out harmless experiments with chemistry sets in their bedrooms.

On the other hand, the position that ordinary citizens, including those who lack backgrounds in the life sciences, should be in a position to conduct unchecked biological studies becomes more problematic when it is applied to biohackers who perform procedures on human tissue. For example, some of the more extreme practitioners, called "grinders" or "bodyhackers," perform minor surgeries on their colleagues, such as implanting magnets in their fingertips so they may sense magnetic fields. Other grinders, using their own bodies as experimental canvases, apply electrical current to their temples so as to stimulate the cerebral cortex and ostensibly reduce anxiety, or inject a serum into their eyes so they may experience night vision temporarily. Critics of the biohacking movement argue that such procedures are questionable at best, especially when their long-term effects have not been established and they are performed by amateurs. When examining the tenets, ethics, and hazards of biohacking, then, it is important to specify the sorts of experiments and interventions that are under discussion, since they vary considerably.

As noted at the outset of this chapter, the majority of biohackers are drawn to the applications of biotechnology, with numerous gene manipulation experiments having been performed by citizen scientists throughout the world in recent years. Some have been carried out in home laboratories, while others have been conducted in "hackerspaces" or "hacklabs," communal workspaces where do-it-yourselfers congregate. Such genetic experimentation, as it happens, is also the branch of citizen science that critics most often single out as a threat to the population. The reason for their concern: the tools of biotechnology not only make it theoretically possible for a biohacker to refashion lethal pathogens by manipulating their genetic codes, pathogens that could then be released into the population, but also because the tools themselves are widely available to the public and relatively inexpensive to acquire.

"You can pick up any recent issue of *Science* magazine, flip through it and find ads for kit after kit of biotechnology techniques," says molecular biologist Tom St. John of the Hutchinson Cancer Research Center in Seattle.[21] Remarkably, St. John made this comment in 1988 in a *Washington Post* article, one titled *Playing God in Your Basement* and likening biohacking to 1970s computer hacking.[22] Since the article's publication, the dissemination of genetic engineering techniques has continued, even accelerated, thanks in part to an economic downturn in the 2000s that prompted several struggling biotech firms to sell off their equipment to biohacker collectives.[23] In some cases, lab equipment was offered on e-commerce sites like Craigslist and eBay, with apparatuses capable of duplicating genetic material being marketed for only a few hundred dollars.[24]

Also galvanizing those do-it-yourself biologists having an interest in biotechnology was the publication of the first draft of the human genome by the International Human Genome Sequencing Consortium. Appearing in the February 2001, issue of the science journal *Nature*, it was rightfully heralded as a profound advancement in human knowledge.[25] At once, the information was seized upon both by professional and do-it-yourself biologists, with the two groups finding it to be of immense value. And this was intended to be the case. "It's a shop manual, with an incredibly detailed blueprint for building every human cell," says Francis Collins, Director of the National Genome Research Institute in Bethesda, Maryland.[26]

Still another important contribution to the biohacking movement came with advances in "synthetic biology," an innovative, interdisciplinary enterprise situated at the intersection of engineering and biology. Synthetic biology brings together biotechnology, genetic engineering, molecular and evolutionary biology, and a handful of other fields in order to create new life forms or modify those that already exist in nature so as to endow them with unique properties and abilities. Unlike cloning, which requires pre-existing or "real" DNA to launch the process of gene duplication, synthetic biology produces DNA from scratch, meaning it is a more versatile and cost-effective means of fabricating genetic material for research purposes. Not surprisingly, it has been a boon to biohackers, with artificial gene synthesis allowing them to obtain mail-order, synthetic DNA at a reasonable price.

So it was that the biohacking movement, fueled by the publication of the human genome together with the accessibility of lab equipment and synthetic DNA, flourished. Like the 1960s and 1970s computer hackers who preceded them, do-it-yourself biologists became increasingly aware of one another and began joining forces on research projects as well as sharing laboratory equipment or pooling their resources so as to purchase it. Clearly, the movement was well on its way.

In 2008, this trend of biohackers coalescing into small groups or tight-knit communities was given a boost with the arrival of "DIYbio" ("Do-it-yourself biology"). A network for biohackers, DIYbio was created, according to Alessandro Delfanti, to provide "non-expert, citizen biologists with a collective environment and cheap and open source tools and protocols for biological research which [could] be conducted in amateur settings."[27] Although the original DIYbio headquarters was based in Boston, groups began popping up in a number of U.S. cities and beyond. Before long, biohackers from around the globe were logging on to the operation's website, *DIYbio.org*, to obtain information and advice as well as to share their experiences. In bringing together thousands of citizen scientists, *DIYbio.org* quickly became, and remains today, one the most significant and influential online networks of its type.

Another important addition to the biohacking scene was "Genspace," the aforementioned community lab in New York City. Founded in 2009, Genspace, which still flourishes today, provides laboratory space and equipment for biohackers, along with courses in synthetic biology and other subjects. And similar to Genspace is the "London Biohackspace," established in 2011. Like other community-based hacklabs, it offers research facilities for do-it-yourself biologists and encourages all manner of individuals to use them, including artists interested in creating bio-art, along with computer programmers and engineers. And then there is the "Hackuarium" in Lausanne, Switzerland, which makes laboratory space available for do-it-yourself biologists to conduct an assortment of projects, such as innovative methods of food production. To be sure, such networks, organizations, and hacklabs serve multiple functions, furnishing meaningful and affordable opportunities for biological experimentation combined with educational programming and peer support. As well, they foster a sense of community and a concomitant sense of personal responsibility.

As to the nature of the biohackers' research projects, they run the gamut from the rudimentary to the relatively sophisticated. In the former category, ambitious bands of biohackers in their teens have concocted everything from "blinking cells to banana-scented bacteria," writes Marcus Wohlson.[28] By comparison, adult hackers in the latter category have taken on medical challenges, as in the design of microscopic agents capable of identifying the presence of pathogens. In one such case, a Venezuelan computer scientist with an interest in biology is working on a diagnostic test for the insect-borne, parasitic disease known as Chagas, his goal being to devise an "off-the-grid diagnostic rapid response kit" that would be compact and low-cost and thus suitable for use by the money-strapped, far-flung villages of Central and South America.[29]

Still another acclaimed cluster of studies entails the insertion of genes into bacteria to make the bacteria glow. Like many experiments that observers misperceive as inconsequential, even silly, these studies may in fact yield considerable benefits for humanity, food safety being one of them. Biohackers explain that such experiments could lead to a modified bacterium that would become luminous upon detecting chemical contaminants, like melamine, in food products, thereby serving as red flags to consumers. "People should have an inexpensive and portable test to make sure their food is safe," says an avid biohacker, a software engineer, who has undertaken such a project. "[N]o lab was working on this, so I said let's do it ourselves."[30]

To obtain a more precise glimpse into citizen scientists' activities, specifically in their preferred area—biotechnology—leaders of the Synthetic Biology Project of the Woodrow Wilson International Center for Scholars administered a self-report questionnaire to biohacker communities.[31] The results, published in 2013, found that of the 359 do-it-yourself biologists who responded to the survey, approximately 65 percent had extracted DNA in their experiments, while nearly 20 percent had created synthetic genes. Over 40 percent of the total sample had genetically engineered a bacterium, with roughly 5 percent having engineered the cell of a mammal. Other types of projects involved protein purification and self-testing for the presence of specific genes. In the opinion of the study's authors, the findings indicate that biohackers, as a whole, possess viable skills and are capable of contributing meaningfully to the life sciences.[32]

Regarding the attributes of these do-it-yourselfers, the same study found that a substantial number was far removed from the popular stereotype of the youthful amateur who tinkers with dodgy microbes in an improvised basement lab. Forty-two percent of the respondents were between thirty-five and forty-five years of age, forty-six percent possessed graduate degrees in subjects ranging from jurisprudence to medicine, and thirty-five percent carried out their experiments in hackerspaces.[33] It would appear, then, that a sizable share of biohackers, at least as measured those willing to respond to the aforementioned survey, are not the untutored eccentrics so often portrayed in media reports.

In terms of biohackers' values, the most strongly embraced entails a respect for, and insistence upon, unrestrained access to information; a reverence, as mentioned earlier, that was prevalent among the 1960s and 1970s computer hackers. Based on the notion that scientific knowledge belongs to all of humanity, this crucial underpinning of the citizen science experience has been a provocative one since the movement emerged, and it still raises the hackles of those who oppose hands-on biology. This is especially the case for those having corporate interests, as evidenced by a game-changing legal battle in 2013 that centered on open-access DNA research. Since the court's decision affected the biohacking movement, which was indirectly drawn into the matter, it will be useful to briefly revisit this pivotal case.

Proprietary Conflicts

As previously noted, the sequencing of the human genome by a global team of researchers (Human Genome Project) was intended to provide scientists with information that would help in their investigations into the genetic components of numerous medical conditions, the ultimate aim of such studies being to more effectively prevent, diagnose, and treat disease. Since the sequencing of the genome was undertaken for the sake of humanity, the draft was made publicly available in 2001, with the final version being released two years later.

A genome contains all of an organism's genes. In the case of the human genome, it is composed of a long strand of DNA molecules that contains an estimated twenty-one thousand individual genes. So whereas the international team of researchers placed the genome itself in the public domain, it would be up to subsequent researchers to locate and identify, or "isolate," the specific genes contained on it. When those in the scientific and biohacking community sought to do this, however, they soon clashed with advocates of intellectual property rights, who argued that corporations' genetic research programs, upon isolating specific gene sequences, should be permitted to patent these genes along with any tests or treatments based on them. And the corporations were willing to go to the mat in order to do so.

Without hesitation, private firms filed thousands of patents in an effort to secure exclusive rights to genes and thus enrich themselves. And it is certainly true that there was a great deal of money to be made. Within twelve months of the draft of the genome appearing in print, bioinformatics professor Richard Belew reported that "[g]enome projects are already generating huge wealth."[34] Yet the rapid emergence of proprietary databases for genetic discoveries, while profitable for the companies that possessed them, carried a downside in that they prevented other researchers from studying the patented genes. The upshot was that the field of genetics suffered, while the costs of certain genetic tests skyrocketed due to the market control afforded by the licenses.

In due course, the matter found its way to the U.S. Supreme Court, which ruled on the exclusivity issue in the landmark case of the Association for Molecular Pathology v. Myriad Genetics, Inc.[35] The crux of the court's decision: a gene cannot be patented because it already exists in nature. While a scientist may isolate a gene carried on the genome, the scientist did not create it. In the same way that an astronomer who discovers a planet does not own the planet, so identifying a gene sequence does not, in itself, grant one possession of it. The court added, however, that "complementary DNA" or c-DNA—an artificial product—can be patented, since it does not exist in nature but instead is assembled in a lab.

As this battle was raging, advocates of intellectual property rights presented a handful of arguments to buttress their case, one of which sought to drag the practice of biohacking into the dispute. Claiming that society would be better served if private entities held exclusive rights to genes, corporate representatives warned that citizen scientists, through open-sourcing, could otherwise gain access to genetic information and use it against society. "[O]pen-source biology could ... prime the arsenals of would-be 'bio-hackers' who might dream of creating, say, a virus that could wipe out half the residents of Manhattan," writes a journalist giving voice to such concerns.[36] Truth be told, the lawyers' prediction was quite a stretch, with biohacking being introduced into the dispute mainly as a scare tactic. Since the publication of the human genome and the plethora of genetic studies that have ensued, there have been no known cases of citizen scientists using this information for devious purposes. All the same, critics of lay biological research, especially that which entails genetic engineering, have continued to voice their anxieties about the practice of biohacking.

Peril or Promise

As should be apparent by this point, attitudes toward do-it-yourself biology cover the spectrum. Proponents argue that citizen scientists, by working openly and cooperatively, are in a position to help solve some of humanity's greatest problems, from air pollution to cancer. Opponents, meanwhile, insist that furnishing the public with potentially dangerous information along with the tools to act on it is the epitome of poor judgment, a path to disaster. It could be argued, of course, that both stances are extreme due to the limitations that currently exist in much do-it-yourself biology. Taken together, though, these polarized positions illustrate the key issues in the debate about the perils and promise of non-traditional biological experimentation.

Arguments Against Biohacking

Those who oppose lay biological research contend that it poses a threat to society, especially when it entails genetic experiments undertaken by self-educated hobbyists. Among such opponents are molecular biologists, geneticists, and other scientists who have accumulated considerable experience in precisely those fields in which many biohackers strive to participate. These critics are not waging a turf war; it is not a case of credentialed scientists jealously guarding their professions from interlopers, with do-it-yourselfers being looked upon as competition. Rather, it is a case of those who have substantial knowledge of, and experience in, a particular field of study pointing out the problems that may arise when this same field is accessed by those having less knowledge and experience, coupled with little or no regulation, guidance, or oversight.

In terms of specific issues, critics have expressed numerous worries about biohacking over the years, with Dustin Holloway recently organizing these concerns into three broad categories. A bioinformatics engineer at the Dana Farber Cancer Institute, Holloway is also a fellow in the Medical Ethics division of Harvard Medical School.[37]

The first set of concerns centers on laboratory safety measures and the fact that citizen scientists, particularly those with little or no training in biology, may not be familiar with standard lab procedures; they may not be acquainted with the protective measures that should be in place even when working with benign microbes. Naturally, this becomes a bigger worry when the stakes are higher—when the microorganisms are infectious, for instance—since the same unfamiliarity may result in the biohacker, and perhaps others, becoming ill and spreading disease.

The second concern pertains to genetically-modified bacteria and viruses. Critics draw attention to the fact that equipment is now available for biohackers to fashion microscopic agents that do not exist in nature, one problem being that certain characteristics of these novel microbes may not be understood, such as their ability to replicate. Accordingly, a citizen scientist might not be able to recognize and contain any unique risks that might arise from, say, an enhanced bacterium. As public policy analyst and author David Bollier has said about studies in which DNA is manipulated, "the 'genetic pollution' that could result from slipshod genetic engineering could be irreversible and calamitous."[38]

Those who oppose biohacking also warn that a do-it-yourselfer could deliberately engineer a dangerous microorganism with which to target specific individuals. In a very real sense, the situation is comparable to the modern-day practice of computer hacking. "Some commentators have noted that 'hacker ethics' did not prevent the masses of malware in the cyber world," says Catherine Jefferson, a researcher at King's College in London.[39] And it is true: the productive experimentation with computer technology that emerged in the 1960s and 1970s was eclipsed by the malicious computer hacking that surged in the 1980s and persists at the present time. It therefore is not unreasonable, nor does it constitute fear-mongering, to predict that a small subset of do-it-yourselfers will eventually break away from the biohacking community and attempt to engineer harmful microbes so as to traumatize or sicken others. Depending on the nature of the microorganisms and their intended effects, such deeds could constitute prosecutable biocrimes.

And third, critics express concern about the prospect of a full-scale bioterrorist attack organized and executed by biohackers, a type of assault designed to frighten the general population while incapacitating or killing a sizable segment of it. Such a development might involve biohackers marketing their services to a domestic terrorist organization or, alternatively, functioning autonomously to intimidate the government or citizenry. "While there is no evidence that DIYbio represents a national security threat of this sort," writes Holloway, "bioterrorism is a risk that policy makers must consider when developing regulations for citizen science."[40]

The bioinformatics engineer adds that the public release of information detailing specific techniques of genetic engineering has contributed to this concern, an issue that Hillary Clinton addressed in 2011 at the Biological Weapons Convention in Geneva while serving as Secretary of State. Acknowledging that the sharing of gene-synthesis information "obviously has many benefits for research," Clinton proceeded to warn that "it could also potentially be used to assemble the components of a deadly organism."[41] Certainly there have been a number of projects over the years that have involved the genetic manipulation of the deadly influenza viruses, a handful of which have ignited worldwide debate over the dangers they pose.

One set of studies was published in 2012 by scientists in the Netherlands, Japan, and the United States, and centered on a man-made microbe, a genetically-modified version of the avian influenza virus.[42] Considered by many in the life sciences to be the most terrifying microbe ever created, far more frightening than Ebola and other naturally-occurring viruses, this particular "supervirus" could kill up to 400,000,000 people if it were to escape from the lab. And it was this unnerving prospect that led to a dispute about the judiciousness of the research.

"This work should never have been done," declares molecular biologist Richard Elbright of Rutgers University.[43] Elbright's opinion is shared by scores of scientists who feel that the studies' disadvantages outweigh their advantages. They argue that while the projects may have helped facilitate the development of treatments for use if the avian virus eventually mutates into a lethal, cross-species agent, the studies themselves, by genetically concocting the threatening supervirus itself, may actually have hastened the probability of a catastrophic event. Equally ill-advised, they add, was the publication of the research procedures in the pages of the journals *Nature, Science*, and *Cell*.

Another series of studies that came out in print in the 1990s and 2000s recounted scientists' reconstruction of the virus that set off the Spanish influenza pandemic in the early twentieth century, an epic contagion that took the lives of fifty million people.[44] The research made use of the original 1918 virus that had been kept frozen in a level-3 biosafety lab, with scientists using the genome to reconstruct the historic microorganism and documenting the process by which they did it. As with the response surrounding the avian flu research, reaction to the Spanish flu studies was stormy, particularly the research team's decision to publicly reveal the nuts and bolts of the gene-sequencing process used to recreate the virus.

"Not surprisingly," writes Jan van Aken, formerly of the Hamburg Centre for Biological Arms Control, "the publication of the Spanish influenza research triggered a controversial debate within, but not exclusive to, the scientific community, as arms-control experts questioned whether it was wise to publish a detailed account of its genome and recipe for resurrection."[45] The latter group, arms-control experts, is composed of specialists in several fields, many of whom are convinced that rogue states are eager to exploit such research and that the publication of the influenza studies unwittingly handed over to these hostile entities the instructions for a biological weapon.

As noted earlier, there is also the apprehension that biohackers could likewise act on descriptive material of this sort. Opponents speculate that one or more do-it-yourself biologists could restore a pathogen of extraordinary virulence, one that could culminate in a pandemic capable of decimating humanity. And it is such hair-raising forecasts that rile advocates of citizen science. "I am really sick and tired of folks waving this particular red flag," says Ellen Jorgensen, the molecular biologist who co-founded Genspace.[46]

Arguments for Biohacking

Jorgensen, a leading supporter of citizen science, is one of several advocates who insist that the trepidation surrounding biohacking is, on the whole, without foundation. Explaining that many of those who engage in home or community-based biological studies have much to offer society through their research, they say it is wrong-headed to attempt to curb, contain, or prohibit biohackers' activities. If anything, these proponents maintain, do-it-yourself biology should be promoted.

Adherents of citizen science also point to historical figures, some of our greatest minds, whose inventions and discoveries in makeshift studios, workshops, and laboratories advanced humanity. Sometimes referred to as "gentleman scientists" in the past, such do-it-yourselfers included inventor and statesman Benjamin Franklin, as well as mathematician and father of the mechanical computer Charles Babbage, and Babbage's close friend and colleague, naturalist Charles Darwin. "Darwin may have been the original do-it-yourself biologist," says bioengineer Drew Endy, "as he didn't originally work for any institution."[47]

Jumping ahead to the early 1970s, Apple Computer co-founders Steve Jobs and Steve Wozniack created their first circuit boards not in a high-tech, corporate workspace but in Wozniack's bedroom and in Jobs' garage. And figuratively linking such early, home-based pursuits to contemporary biohacking is fellow computer aficionado, Microsoft's Bill Gates, who recently stated that, if younger, he would be among today's biohackers.[48] "If you want to change the world in some big way," says Gates in a *Wired* interview, "that's where you should start—biological molecules."[49] So while a case could be made that biohacking is different from most other do-it-yourself endeavors in that it has the potential to cause harm to others, even to the population at large, the basic argument itself is beyond dispute: monumental discoveries and inventions have been made, and will continue being made, by people besides those credentialed figures working in conventional academic and industrial settings.

Then, too, proponents of biohacking point out to those having concerns about the practice that it is not necessarily within the expertise of citizen scientists to carry out cutting-edge genetic research, as in the reconstruction of the 1918 influenza virus. And even if they do possess the requisite skills, the equipment that is presently available for use in alternative labs might well be inadequate for such radical tasks. "It's misguided to think that everything that a professional lab can do will also be possible in a home setting," says Jason Bobe, director of Harvard University's Personal Genome Project.[50] To date, the potentially transformative genetic projects that citizen scientists have undertaken have proven to be largely unsuccessful, although this could change in the years ahead.

As for the worry that those involved in hands-on biology will stage a bioterror attack, supporters of the biohacking movement explain that large-scale biological aggression is far more difficult to execute than is commonly believed. Accordingly, it would most likely be perpetrated by a hostile nation or a well-funded terrorist organization, not by a biohacker or a team of hackers. Finally, regarding laboratory accidents and calculated biocrimes, advocates call attention to the fact that a progressive segment of the biohacker community is championing the adoption of educational and self-regulatory guidelines to help ensure that biohacking remains safe and legal. Of course, given the libertarian principles held by a sizable portion of the community, it should not come as a surprise that some biohackers firmly reject this idea, their objection being that it violates the essence of the do-it-yourself experience. Others contend, however, that such measures could help stave off a far more intrusive development, namely the imposition of government protocols and the monitoring of home and community-based labs by state and federal officials.

As it stands, biohackers in Europe are already barred from operating informal genetics laboratories without a license, a prohibition that has not been enacted in the United States. "In America," reports *The Economist*, "the FBI has opted for a more enlightened approach."[51] It is one that operates on the astute assumption that the governmental policing of biohackers would almost certainly drive a substantial share of them underground, presumably the most dubious. Accordingly, the FBI has taken a different course: it permits citizen scientists to conduct biological research without formal scrutiny. Equally progressive, it looks upon them as potential allies in the "war on terror" and seeks their collaboration since they are singularly well-placed to assist in foiling biocrimes and bioterror operations. As Marcus Wohlsen puts it, those in the biohacking community are "the eyes and ears in the best position to know if one of their own [begins] veering the wrong way."[52]

In terms of the FBI's carefully calibrated entry into the world of citizen science, it began in the summer of 2006 with the establishment of the Weapons of Mass Destruction Directorate, or WMDD. The directorate, which still exists today, is composed of representatives from the fields of intelligence and law enforcement in consort with experts in biological, chemical, and nuclear weaponry, with its mission being to oversee federal investigations into impending attacks that involve weapons of mass destruction. To this end, the directorate interfaces not only with governmental and industrial entities, but also with the biohacker community.

A document from the WWMD explains its function as it pertains to citizen scientist groups.[53] "These groups believe advances in science and biotechnology, just like the computer revolution, can be pursued in a home garage or community meeting place and outside of traditional academic and industrial settings," reads the document. "WMDD operates an initiative to develop partnerships with the amateur biology community in order to garner their assistance in preventing, detecting, and responding to incidents of misuse, particularly for nefarious purposes."[54]

The agency accomplishes this task by referring biohackers to the WMD Coordinator if they wish to report suspicious activities, a situation that might arise if a do-it-yourselfer had reason to believe that a fellow hacker was engineering a microbe to be used in a bioterror attack. Yet the directorate's connection to the biohacking community extends beyond the reporting of possible criminal activity to encompass relationship-building events and educational offerings as well. For instance, the WMDD assists do-it-yourself biologists with security and safety issues, while groups like DIYbio and Genspace, in turn, welcome representatives of the directorate to their facilities and enlighten them about various aspects of hands-on biology. It seems that many biohackers consider it a smart move to the work with the directorate; that it is to the movement's benefit to help prevent mischief, since, if one of its own were to engage in a harmful stunt, it could stigmatize the entire do-it-yourself community and cause external constraints to be placed upon all biohackers.

That said, this alliance with the FBI is not without its share of detractors both at home and abroad. The prominent German biohacker Rudiger Trojok, for one, has gone so far as to compare the agency's presence to that of the Stasi in the former East Germany, the tyrannical secret police who intruded into every aspect of citizens' lives.[55] And yet, such differences of opinion notwithstanding, it seems the American biohacker community largely accepts the FBI's nominal involvement, while the federal agency appears to have developed genuine respect for the citizen science movement itself. Considering that those who engage in hands-on biology have thus far conducted themselves in a responsible, conscientious manner, it is understandable that they have earned the agency's approbation. And this brings us to the subject of biohacker ethics.

In 2011, DIYbio held a series of meetings in various cities, the purpose being to devise a code of ethics for North American biohackers in conjunction with one for those in Europe. Drafts of the two codes were published in 2013 and have since come to attract adherents in numerous citizen science networks and organizations.[56] For the most part, the documents reflect the state of biohackers' values, principles, and standards of conduct in Western nations.

Both codes share five core concepts, specifically, the need for biohackers to understand and engage in safe laboratory practices, share research data and other information and knowledge, use their research projects solely for peaceful purposes, practice and advocate for open access to information and decentralized biotechnological research, and help educate the public about biotechnology's benefits for humanity. The North American code further stresses the inherent value of "tinkering," depicting it as spirited experimentation capable of leading to meaningful scientific advances. It also calls for citizen scientists to be respectful of the environment. More extensive and in some ways superior is the European ethical code, which adds that citizen scientists should be aware of their own limitations, responsive to the concerns of the community, accountable for their actions, and respectful of all forms of life.

In their emphasis on autonomy, open access, shared knowledge, and peaceful and productive experimentation, both the North American and European codes harken back to the "hacker ethic" of the 1960s and 1970s computer enthusiasts. And like the original hackers whose inspired tinkering changed the world in positive respects, so may biohackers, with greater expertise and more sophisticated equipment, eventually do the same.

As for those harboring sinister motives, such malicious do-it-yourselfers will almost certainly materialize sooner or later. To suggest otherwise is naïve. Humanity has always contained a destructive component, a bad seed that invariably manifests itself, and there is no reason to believe the realm of citizen science will somehow be immune. In terms of the extent to which this rogue element will cause significant biological harm, it remains to be seen, just as it is not yet known how the biohacker community will respond to such a disturbing turn of events. Until that time, however, sustained networking by biohackers, together with the internalization and promotion of meaningful ethical standards and a constructive, respectful relationship with law enforcement appears to be the most judicious course of action.

◆ 4 ◆

Pathogens, Toxins and Their Weaponization
Science Subverted

The number of microorganisms that cause disease in humans is substantial—an estimated 1,400 viruses, bacteria, and protozoa have been identified thus far—but only a small subset is believed to appeal to prospective bioterrorists.[1] Even so, it is a subset that carries the potential to inflict all manner of harm on the human population. To rank the degree of hazard such agents and their toxins pose to national security, the Centers for Disease Control and Prevention has created three broad classifications for use by public health and biodefense organizations. Known as Biodefense Categories A, B, and C, they pertain to a pathogenic agent's characteristics and capabilities, as well as to society's ability to act in response to its appearance in the population.[2]

In this chapter, the CDC's classification scheme is examined, including a sampling of those entities that constitute each of the categories and their means of transmission, symptoms, and mortality rates. In several instances, relevant bioterrorism-related issues are highlighted as well. Subsequent to this, the coverage explores the current methods, as well as the challenges, of transforming a biological agent into a viable weapon.

Pathogens and Toxins

Biodefense Category A

The pathogenic organisms and toxins that comprise Category A present the greatest threat to the nation's biosecurity. These are agents that have high mortality rates and can be spread effortlessly from person to person (e.g., plague) or easily disseminated through other means (e.g., anthrax). Most also carry the potential for airborne transmission. In addition, they place an immense burden on public health agencies in that they require special action, even extraordinary measures in some cases. And because they are easily transmitted and deadly, their mere appearance in the population promises to trigger alarm and create social havoc—an objective of terrorists of all stripes. Six such biological agents and the diseases they produce are discussed below, beginning with anthrax, the bacterium that was deployed in the bioterror campaign that followed the attacks on the World Trade Center and the Pentagon on September 11, 2001.

Anthrax. Among the pathogens that bioterrorism experts consider to be the most formidable is *Bacillus anthracis*, the agent that causes anthrax infection. Long regarded as a high-probability bioweapon, it is one of the likeliest pathogens to be used in a future bio-offensive.

While practically anyone, anywhere, could be exposed to anthrax in the course of a bioterror attack, some people, by virtue of their occupations or circumstances, are at a greater risk of exposure. These include members of the military, as well as postal workers who may come into contact with the bacterium in the course of a mail-related bioterror attack. Also at risk are men and women whose work puts them in contact with certain types of animals, with veterinarians, ranchers, and farm hands falling into such occupational categories. Laboratory workers also may have reason for concern, specifically those who are assigned to biosafety labs. And individuals who inject heroin have an elevated risk of infection, with anthrax cases recently emerging among injectable drug users in Scotland, England, Denmark, and Germany. In these incidents, it is suspected that the drugs were contaminated with anthrax spores. If so, it is plausible that heroin consumers could also contract the infection by smoking or snorting the tainted product.

The pathogen *B. anthracis* is spread through four different routes. First, it can enter the body when a person inhales, which leads to "pulmonary" or "inhalation anthrax." The most lethal form of the infection and therefore one that might appeal to bioterrorists, the microorganism is pulled deep into the lungs, where it lodges. As to the initial indicators, they resemble those found in other infections: flu-like symptoms, most notably a mild fever, muscle stiffness and achiness, fatigue, headache, and upset stomach. In some cases, sore throat may be present as well, along with chest discomfort and hemoptysis (i.e., coughing up blood). Shortly thereafter, the person may experience a period of outward improvement that lasts a day or two before suffering a sudden, final collapse, during which the individual's fever climbs sharply and the person finds it difficult to breathe. The illness may culminate in shock due to decreased blood flow. Meningitis or respiratory failure may result, too. While the U.S. Food and Drug Administration reports that untreated inhalation anthrax is fatal at least eighty percent of the time, the affliction, on the upside, cannot be spread from person to person.[3]

The second mode of anthrax infection is gastrointestinal, and like other forms of the illness, is rare. Gastrointestinal anthrax is caused by eating the raw or undercooked meat from an infected animal, and it is fatal between twenty-five and seventy-percent of the time in the absence of antibiotic therapy.[4] Symptoms may include fever, sore throat, swelling of the neck, severe abdominal pain, vomiting, gastrointestinal bleeding, diarrhea, hematemesis (i.e., vomiting of blood), and hematochezia (i.e., blood in stools). As with inhalation anthrax, the condition is not contagious.

The third route of infection occurs when the pathogen enters the body through an abrasion, sore, or cut on the skin, and is termed "cutaneous anthrax." The most common and most treatable form of the infection, cutaneous anthrax is characterized by itching at the site, along with swollen or tender lymph nodes near the region and a patch on the skin that progresses to a bump. This, in turn, develops into a large black sore, one the victim may initially mistake for a spider bite. Unlike other forms of the infection, cutaneous anthrax can be spread from person to person if direct contact is made with the lesion. Fortunately, the condition is readily treatable with antibiotics, with the mortality rate in such cases estimated to be twenty percent.[5]

The final route of infection is "injection anthrax" and occurs when an individual injects drugs, thus far heroin, contaminated with anthrax spores. "Symptoms may be similar to those of cutaneous anthrax," reads a CDC précis on the subject, "but there may be infection deep under the skin or in the muscle where the drug was injected."[6] For this reason, it may be difficult to recognize the condition in its early stages, a period when the bacterium, because it was injected, spreads rapidly throughout the body. And not only can the initial diagnosis be tricky; treatment of injectable anthrax often requires surgery, according to physicians in Germany familiar with its course of treatment.[7] Regarding the mortality rate, it is estimated to be thirty percent with treatment.[8] To date, no cases of injection anthrax have been reported in the United States.

Botulism. Another potential tool of those seeking to incapacitate a segment of the population is the bacterium *Clostridium botulinum*, an agent that produces several neurotoxins, four of which—toxins A, B, E, and F—sicken or kill humans. "Botulinum toxin A is the most toxic substance known to mankind," says Walter Biederbick, Head of the Centre for Biological Security at the Robert Koch Institute in Berlin.[9] Virtually anyone can be exposed to the entity that results in botulism, with injectable drug users being at a higher risk for a particular form of it, one known as *wound botulism.*[10] In this type, an injection site, most often that of a black tar heroin user, becomes infected.[11] Other forms include *foodborne botulism,* brought about by eating bacteria-tainted food and colloquially referred to as "food poisoning"; *infant botulism*, which affects those under one year of age; and a man-made version of the illness known as *inhalation botulism*.

Regarding their distinguishing properties, the foodborne variety is associated with preserved foods that are low in acid, like canned corn or beets, and those that are inadequately prepared, such as fish, ham, or sausage that has been undercooked or processed improperly. With prompt anti-toxin treatment, the mortality rate for foodborne botulism is five to ten percent, although this figure climbs to nearly fifty percent if the condition remains untreated or if the anti-toxin is delayed, according to the World Health Organization and a USAMRIID study.[12]

In terms of the remaining forms of the infection, infant botulism is by far the most common type in the United States and comes about when an infant ingests *C. botulinum* spores, which may be present in soil, honey, corn syrup, and other products. Once the spores have been consumed, they germinate in the gut and produce toxins. (The adult immune system is able to detect these spores and prevent them from germinating). Fortunately, the mortality rate for infant botulism is very low, since those who contract the infection are nearly always hospitalized and treated in a timely manner. In this respect, the condition is different from the remaining form of the illness, one having a potentially astronomical mortality rate.

This last type, inhalation botulism, is linked exclusively to bioterrorism and requires that the bacterium be intentionally aerosolized. It is this process that increases its lethality exponentially. "Some authors have estimated that as little as 1 g of aerosolized [Botulinum neurotoxin] could lead to the death of over 1.5 million people," says McGill University neurologist Colin Chalk.[13] Accordingly, the prospect of a bioterror organization creating an airborne variety of botulism is one of the principal apprehensions of those whose responsibility is biodefense.

As for the clinical presentations of the two types of botulism that bioterrorists might deploy, foodborne and inhalation, they are largely identical, with neurotoxins in both forms producing an acute paralytic condition. Symptoms may include vertigo, ptosis (i.e., drooping eyelids), visual anomalies, dilated pupils, slurred speech, difficulty swallowing, and descending flaccid paralysis.[14] Since the neurotoxins block nerve functions and prevent muscle contraction, the muscles become unresponsive and limp, with the body assuming a floppy appearance.[15] In foodborne botulism, additional symptoms typically consist of abdominal cramps, nausea, vomiting, and diarrhea. Regardless of the route of infection, though, botulism, particularly if anti-toxins are not administered rapidly after the onset of symptoms, may culminate in respiratory paralysis and death.

Although *C. botulinum* is available in nature, it nevertheless remains a challenge for potential bioterrorists to obtain the particular strain that produces neurotoxins most easily and efficiently.[16] That said, if the perpetrators did succeed in acquiring the desired strain, instructions are available on the Internet that would help guide them through the reproduction of the neurotoxins.

Ebola and Marburg. Another set of diseases that invites the concern of biodefense experts are two that, until recently, were designated "Hemorrhagic Fevers." Today they are known as Ebola Virus Disease (EVD) and Marburg Virus Disease (MVD), and are acute afflictions caused by filoviruses, one of four families of pathogens that produce often-fatal hemorrhagic conditions. The remaining families consist of arenaviruses (e.g., Lassa Fever), bunyaviruses (e.g., Hantavirus Pulmonary Syndrome), and flaviviruses (e.g., Dengue Fever).

Individuals who are at the greatest risk of contracting Ebola or Marburg are those who live or work in regions of Africa that have endured recent outbreaks of the diseases, along with researchers and lab technicians in other parts of the world who conduct research on animals exported from such areas or from the Philippines. At heightened risk, too, are those who provide care to family members or others who are suffering from EVD or MVD, and those who prepare the bodies of the casualties.

As for transmission, infection occurs when a person makes contact with the blood or bodily fluids of a person suffering from Ebola or Marburg, or with the sufferer's items that have been contaminated by these substances. Although it has not yet been confirmed, sexual contact, particularly male to female contact, is also suspected of being a route of infection.[17] Less often, transmission occurs through contact with an infected primate, such as when butchering, cooking, or eating it. Regarding airborne transmission, an international team of scientists studying an Ebola outbreak in Africa in 2015 raised the possibility that the virus could eventually mutate into an airborne agent, adding that it is probably already spreading by this route in certain instances. "It is very likely that at least some degree of Ebola virus transmission currently occurs via infectious aerosols generated from the gastrointestinal tract, the respiratory tract, or medical procedures," reports the team.[18] Even so, the pathogen continues to be classified as a blood-borne agent, not as an airborne entity, with the World Health Organization maintaining its stance that the virus is unlikely to mutate into a form that permits significant airborne transmission in the foreseeable future.[19] Lastly, it should be noted that neither Ebola nor Marburg is spread through the water supply.

Although these two diseases are comparable in presentation, an important difference exists between Ebola and Marburg in terms of their mortality rates. The WHO estimates the death rate for Ebola to be ninety percent, whereas that of Marburg ranges from twenty-four to eighty-eight percent.[20]

It is believed that recent advances in the treatment of Ebola will reduce its elevated mortality rate, although it remains to be seen the extent to which they may do so.

Concerning the symptoms, both conditions, the presentations of which may vary from person to person, begin abruptly with the virus targeting the immune system. Initial features include fever, headache, muscle stiffness and cramps, nausea and vomiting, and profound weakness.[21] Sore throat may be present as well. In EVD, this period is referred to as the "dry phase," during which diagnosis may be difficult since the symptoms are not unique to hemorrhagic fever. A few days later, however, additional symptoms emerge and are more telling, such as a rash on the individual's back and chest along with a blank expression in the eyes, since the virus is now affecting the nervous system, including the brain. Finally, multiple organ systems become implicated, blood vessels become damaged, and the body becomes unable to regulate itself. Severe hemorrhaging may result in massive internal bleeding, with blood loss also occurring through the eyes, body orifices, and sites of injections. Death occurs within a day or two of the onset of this last cluster of symptoms, known as the "hemorrhagic syndrome."[22]

Here it should be noted that a person suffering from Ebola or Marburg Virus Disease may not experience hemorrhaging, despite the popular image of the afflictions. "Typically, the Ebola virus leads to hemorrhagic syndrome about 30 percent to 50 percent of the time," says microbiologist Angela Rasmussen.[23] Those infected by the Marburg virus do not necessarily progress to a hemorrhagic stage either, although when this does occur, it usually happens a few days later than is the case with Ebola.

Unfortunately, neither EVD nor MVD are treatable with antiviral drugs. Instead, treatment is supportive and instituted in response to the emergence of specific symptoms. In nearly all cases, such measures include fluid replacement while also addressing secondary infections as they emerge. Depending on the symptom presentation and the availability of medical facilities, they may also involve blood transfusions, kidney dialysis, and other interventions. Encouragingly, several treatments are currently in development, as is a vaccine, SV-EBOV, for Ebola Virus Disease.[24]

As bioterror agents, Ebola or Marburg could be devastating, although it would be difficult to weaponize and deploy either pathogen. That said, this did not stop the Japanese religious sect, Aum Shinrikyo, from acquiring samples of the Ebola virus for use in its bioterrorism research. "In 1992," writes Dina Maron in *Scientific American*, "they sent a medical group of 40 people ostensibly to help provide aid during an Ebola outbreak in the Democratic Republic of the Congo."[25] The true reason: to snatch vials containing the virus. Luckily for the Japanese population, the sect's subsequent Ebola studies were never completed.

Plague. Another prospective bioterror agent that has, for centuries, terrified the human race is that which causes plague. A bacterium known as *Yersinia pestis*, the pathogen is most often found in rats, chipmunks, prairie dogs, and the fleas that feed on them. When these animals, in turn, bite humans or other animals, the infection is transmitted, with the result being the grave illness known as *bubonic plague*. Fortunately, the disease rarely spreads from person to person, and it seldom occurs in Western nations. On the other hand, the pathogen that causes bubonic plague, if the infection remains untreated, may multiply in the bloodstream and cause *septicemic plague*, or it may travel to the lungs to produce *pneumonic plague*. And what is most significant about the latter condition, also known as *inhalation plague*, is that it can be transmitted to others when an infected individual coughs or sneezes, thereby causing the bacterium to become airborne. And this is a deadly matter. Whereas untreated bubonic plagues carries a fifty percent mortality rate, that for untreated pneumonic plague approaches one hundred percent.[26] Bioterrorism and biowarfare experts agree that pneumonic plague would present a significant threat to the human population.[27]

As it stands, the chances of a person contracting any form of the plague through natural means is extremely low, with a very small number of cases being reported annually, mostly in Africa. All the same, those who live or work in rural or semi-rural areas of the United States, enjoy camping as a hobby, or, like veterinarians, work with animals, do face a minuscule risk.

The symptom presentations of the three forms of plague differ in important respects. In bubonic plague, a dark eruption occurs at the site of the bite within a week, accompanied by profound swelling of nearby lymph nodes. The victim next experiences fever and chills, while purple blotches begin to appear on the body, the consequence of hemorrhaging beneath the skin. As the condition progresses and impacts the nervous system, various neurological and psychological anomalies may occur.[28]

The above-mentioned symptoms are in contrast to those produced by septicemic plague, in which the victim breaks out in a rash and dies within twenty-four hours. "This form of plague is always fatal," Mike Ibeji says of the septicemic variety, "but very rare because it is flea-borne and the victim is usually dead before transmission can occur."[29]

The third form of plague, pneumonic, is of greatest concern to those in the realm of biodefense. Despite the fact that it is the least common form of the disease, it presents the most serious threat due to its transmissibility. Then, too, antibiotic therapy must be initiated within twenty-four hours of symptom onset or the victim is unlikely to survive.

In terms of its clinical presentation, pneumonic plague manifests abruptly with weakness, high fever, headache, nausea, and vomiting, as well as with breathing difficulties and a cough, often containing blood. Within forty-eight hours, the patient may go into shock, and respiratory failure may lead to the person's demise. While the Black Death, which killed fifty million Europeans and a total of 200,000,000 people worldwide in the fourteenth century, has traditionally believed to have been the bubonic plague, medical historians have recently raised the possibility that pneumonic plague may have played an important role in the epic contagion owing to its extremely swift spread. Such is its profound virulence.

Smallpox. Extremely virulent, too, is smallpox. A scourge that was officially eradicated worldwide in 1980, biodefense experts warn that if terrorists were to obtain and deploy the fearsome pathogen, the ensuing contagion could sicken or kill millions as it has done in the past. Certainly it is true that the ancient disease, which is caused by the *variola virus*, has decimated human populations over the past three millennia, with smallpox having a mortality rate of thirty percent and being easily transmitted. "In the past, natural smallpox was usually spread through close contact of less than 6 feet, with an infected individual spreading aerosolized viral particles, or through contaminated clothing or bed linens," says Jennifer Brower of the RAND Corporation. "There were occasional cases of transmission over larger distances," she adds.[30] For these reasons—and because most medical professionals today have no experience diagnosing smallpox, a disease for which there is still no treatment—the variola virus would constitute a daunting biological weapon.

Regarding its symptoms, smallpox begins with a prodromal phase characterized by high fever (101–104° Fahrenheit), malaise, headache, muscle cramps, and occasionally nausea. In the ensuing stage, which manifests a few days later, a rash appears in the mouth and tongue, spreading to the face, limbs, and other parts of the body, and then turning into fluid-filled bumps. "People often say the bumps feel like BB pellets in the skin," reads a CDC description of the disease.[31] Still later, the bumps or pustules develop a crust, fall off, and leave behind the disease's telltale scars on the skin.

Three additional forms of smallpox exist besides the conventional type. These consist of "modified smallpox," a less severe form that occurs in those who have been previously vaccinated; "malignant smallpox," in which the lesions are flattened rather than raised, a condition that is associated with an impaired immune system and has a high mortality rate; and "hemorrhagic smallpox," in which bleeding occurs through the skin and mucous membranes. This form, too, is the result of a defective immune system and is usually fatal.

Fortunately, there does exist an effective vaccine against smallpox. And while there is no specific treatment for the disease other than supportive care, administering the vaccine to an individual who has been exposed to the virus may be effective if symptoms have not yet emerged. In addition, ongoing research on oral antiviral medications is yielding encouraging results.

In terms of biological aggression, efforts have already been made to weaponize the smallpox virus, most notably by the USSR prior to its dissolution. This is one reason that governments around the world have destroyed their stockpiles of the pathogen—to prevent its weaponization should it fall into the wrong hands—with the only remaining samples being housed in two high-security research facilities in Russia and the United States.[32] That said, recent genetic-engineering research protocols that entail synthesizing the smallpox virus (i.e., reconstructing it from scratch) present a cause for concern. Drastically limiting the world's stockpiles of the dangerous microbe while, at the same time, permitting laboratories to reconstruct it strikes many biodefense experts as counterintuitive. "The problem is that we have got a lot of people with a lot more talent working in biological laboratories around the world and a lot of them are very well-trained and the potential for mischief here is much greater," says Donald Henderson, Dean Emeritus of the Johns Hopkins School of Public Health.[33] Henderson is also the former director of the World Health Organization's global smallpox eradication program.

Tularemia. More treatable than smallpox is tularemia, a bacterial infection that targets small mammals, but which humans can contract through contact with wild animals or from insect bites. In many cases, mammals, like rabbits, become infected, then spread the pathogen to other species. In other instances, tick and deer fly bites are the means of infection, as is the handling of infected animals. As could be predicted, hunters, veterinarians, and others having exposure to animals are at an elevated risk for the disease.

The causative agent of the disease, *Francisella tularensis*, can enter the human body through mucous membranes or impaired skin, and can also be contracted by eating contaminated food or drinking tainted water. Of greatest concern to biodefense experts, however, is infection by inhalation. "The organism is dangerous because it can be released as an aerosol to cause large tularemia epidemics in both human and animal populations at the same time," says biologist Amy Kraft. "*F. tularensis* is extremely infectious in humans, requiring inhalation of only ten to fifty organisms to cause severe, incapacitating, and sometimes fatal results."[34]

As to symptoms, there are half a dozen tularemia syndromes, all of which typically commence with a cluster of symptoms that include the sudden onset of high fever accompanied by muscle and joint pain, coughing, headache, and fatigue. Depending on the syndrome in question, the infection may spread to the lymph nodes or, if the pathogen enters the bloodstream, it may impact the internal organs and skeletal muscles. Fortunately, treatments are available and the mortality rate is comparatively low. All the same, the illness can be a long and uncomfortable one, and as an epidemic it could deliver a substantial blow to the population, this being among the reasons that experts warn that it would make an attractive bioweapon.

Biodefense Category B

The pathogenic microbes that make up Category B constitute less of a national biosecurity threat than do those contained in Category A, yet they may still pose a problem for society. These are agents that have low mortality rates but high incidence rates, meaning they may not kill their victims but can nevertheless sicken a substantial portion of the population. In addition, the pathogens and toxins are fairly easy to disseminate. And while Category B agents do not call for the exceptional public health measures like those in Category A, they do require that the CDC place increased emphasis on ensuring the accuracy of its identification and diagnostic procedures, while also stepping up its disease surveillance measures.

Category B contains over twice as many pathogenic agents as Category A, with the entities themselves being a rather diverse lot. From mosquito-borne pathogens like the *St. Louis Encephalitis Virus*, they extend to water- and foodborne bacteria, viruses, protozoa, and fungi, such as the pathogenic *Escherichia coli* (*E. coli*), *listeria monocytogenes,* noroviruses, and the *Shigella* bacterium. This classification also contains the microorganisms that produce typhoid fever, glanders, and brucellosis. As for the trio of Category B diseases to be examined below, they consist of Q fever, salmonellosis, and West Nile viral infection. (It should be noted that West Nile infection is contained in Category B of the bioterrorism classification system of the National Institute of Allergy and Infectious Diseases (NIAID) rather than that of the CDC. The two government agencies maintain their own categories of potential bioterror agents, with considerable overlap.)

Q fever. The illness known as *Q fever—Query Fever*, formally—is brought about by *Coxiella burnetii,* a bacterium transmitted through the secretions of sheep, goats, and cattle. Humans contract it by drinking the milk from an animal that carries the pathogen or, more often, by inhaling contaminated air in the vicinity of such animals. The human population is extremely susceptible to *Coxiella burnetii,* with only a tiny number of organisms being sufficient to infect a person; a feature that could make it a desirable tool for bioterrorists.

At greatest risk of infection are those who live in rural areas or, like farmers and many veterinarians, have routine contact with barnyard animals. Also at risk are cattle ranchers, workers at meat processing plants, and researchers who conduct animal research. Regarding the mortality rate, it is, of course, zero for those in whom Q fever is asymptomatic, low for those having the acute form of the malady (<2 percent), and higher for that small portion whose condition progresses to the chronic form of the ailment. According to French biologist Didier Raoult, the death rate for the latter group is between one and eleven percent.[35]

As could be expected, the clinical presentation differs in the malady's acute and chronic forms. Symptoms of the former consist of headache, sensitivity to light, myalgia, high fever, nausea, and chest and abdominal pain. In some cases of acute Q fever, complications set in and may involve the liver, lungs, or brain, most often in the form of hepatitis, pneumonia, or meningitis, respectively. Worse still are the symptoms of the ailment's chronic form, in which the infection recurs several months or years later with a reemergence of the aforementioned features coupled with complications such as bone infection or infective endocarditis, an inflammation of the lining of the heart's chambers and a condition that may necessitate cardiac surgery. For both the acute and chronic types of Q fever, antibiotic therapy is the treatment of choice.

Salmonellosis. An illness that, while unpleasant for the sufferer, usually does not require antibiotics or other measures is salmonellosis, which, like botulism, is often referred to as "food poisoning." Most often caused by the bacterium *Salmonella enterica* (*S. enterica*), a species of the *Salmonella* genus, this pathogen is responsible for nearly 1.4 million cases of food poisoning in the United States each year.[36] The principal risk group: children under five years of age, although anyone may contract the infection, particularly the elderly or those with compromised immune systems.

In humans, transmission of *S. enterica* occurs when a person eats the products of an infected animal, such as milk or eggs, or food made from such an animal, like pigs or poultry. Less frequently, the ingestion of contaminated green vegetables may expose one to the microorganism, while in other instances tainted water is the route of infection.

As to the clinical presentation, it is usually one of fever, abdominal cramps, nausea, vomiting, and diarrhea; a cluster of symptoms that emerge twelve to thirty-six hours after exposure and lasts up to a week. Antibiotic therapy is seldom required for salmonellosis, although severe cases may necessitate hospitalization, particularly if diarrhea leads to dehydration. In such a circumstance, electrolyte replacement and rehydration may become necessary.

As an agent of bioterrorism, salmonella offers certain advantages. Because it sickens rather than kills, it is an ideal agent for alarming a population, causing physical discomfort, and triggering social disruption, but without committing mass murder. The pathogen is also a pragmatic entity, one that can be introduced rather easily into the food supply. Illustrating its viability, Chapter Six contains a case study in which the salmonella bacterium was slipped into salad bars in an Oregon town, an act of domestic sabotage that caused over seven hundred illnesses.

West Nile Virus. The final Category B agent to be examined is a one that has received considerable media attention in recent years, the *West Nile Virus* (WNV), which made its unwelcome U.S. debut in 1999 at the Bronx Zoo. An insect-borne pathogen, it is spread to humans and animals most often by mosquitoes. In terms of risk groups, the chances of contracting the infection is greatest for those who live in regions having large mosquito populations or whose work or hobbies take them outdoors. As for those who do become infected, the chances that their conditions will progress to the more dangerous West Nile Neuroinvasive Disease is increased if they suffer from hypertension, cancer, or kidney disease. And there are additional contributors. "[D]iabetes, as well as older age and male sex, appears to be a significant risk factor for development of WNV neuroinvasive disease," writes research scientist Cynthia M. Jean of the California Department of Public Health.[37]

Concerning the presentation and course of the illness, West Nile infection produces no symptoms, or only negligible ones, in seventy to eighty percent of the cases.[38] The remaining twenty percent may experience fever, aching muscles and joints, rash, and diarrhea, but the symptoms usually do not require medical intervention and subside within a few days. Even so, the person may continue to experience weakness for several months. Unfortunately, in one percent of West Nile infections the individual develops a serious condition, as noted above, which may come to include encephalitis (i.e., inflammation of the brain) or meningitis (i.e., inflammation of the protective membranes, or meninges, that cover the brain and spinal cord). Additional features may consist of tremor, partial paralysis, seizures, stupor, or coma. Death results in a minute percentage of the cases.

As a potential bioweapon, WNV has its advantages and its drawbacks, according to Eric Croddy, analyst at the U.S. Pacific Command in Pearl Harbor. Perhaps its primary advantage is its fairly straightforward weaponization. The virus "could be spread by infecting animal hosts, harvesting mosquitoes that carry the virus, and releasing these insects upon densely population areas," he writes.[39] A significant disadvantage, however, has to do with the effects of this process. They remain largely unknown at this time, with scientists having yet to determine the long-term impact of the microbe's recent arrival on U.S shores. "From the bioweaponeer's perspective," says Croddy, "it is unclear how many infections among targeted populations would result, to what degree infections could be sustained, and whether or not the whole exercise would be worth the expenditure of time and resources."[40] Regardless, West Nile remains on the NIAID's list of possible bioweapons, and, like other potential agents, could, at least in theory, be genetically modified to produce a WNV variant with enhanced adaptability and virulence, thereby making it a stronger, more reliable candidate for inflicting harm on a population.

Biodefense Category C

The third and final classification, Category C, contains those pathogenic agents that have recently emerged or re-emerged in the human population and which cause infectious diseases. Bioterrorism experts suggest that terrorists could convert these pathogens into bioweapons, even though there is no reason to believe that they have an interest in doing so at this time. And because this has not yet happened—and because there is no compelling reason to believe it will occur anytime soon—only thumbnail sketches of a handful of such agents will be presented at this juncture. Suffice it to say, they concern the U.S. biodefense community because they are obtainable, capable of being weaponized, able to be widely disseminated with relative ease, and, in some cases, carry high mortality rates. As such, they could significantly impact a population's health and well-being if a bioterror organization were to decide to exploit them.

Since the late 1960s, researchers have identified over fifty new infectious agents, according to medical geneticist Jianli Dong, who offers several reasons why such pathogens arrive suddenly in the human population or, alternatively, dramatically increase their earlier presence.[41]

> Some of the conditions favoring emergence include human behavior (eg, cyclosporiasis), new technical products (eg, toxic shock syndrome), blood transfusion (eg, hepatitis C virus), movement of exotic animals (eg, monkeypox), nosocomial transmission creating large outbreaks (eg, Ebola hemorrhagic fever), deforestation (eg, Venezuelan hemorrhagic fever), and increased populations of reservoir and vector species (eg, white-tailed deer and *Amblyomma americanum* ticks transmitting human monocytotropic ehrlichiosis).[42]

In other cases, the microorganisms have been around for centuries and have undoubtedly caused illness in humans, but they remained unidentified until recent scientific advances made their detection possible.

Among the pathogens that are contained in Category C is the human coronavirus, dubbed SARS-CoV, the microbe that produces the Severe Acute Respiratory Syndrome (SARS). This disease, which brings on a ferocious form of pneumonia, first appeared in China in 2002 and was formally recognized by the international scientific community in 2003. That same year, a small number of U.S. residents contracted the infection as well.

A similar Category C pathogen is responsible for the Middle East Respiratory Syndrome (MERS), a viral illness that made its debut in Saudi Arabia in 2012, before blazing across the Arabian Peninsula. This acute respiratory ailment, which is caused by the human coronavirus MERS-CoV, reached the United States in May 2014. Although the number of U.S. cases has remained very low, the virus is still propagating and circulating in the Middle East despite ambitious public health efforts to contain it, according to Hamid Y. Hussain of the Dubai Health Authority.[43] And this is worrisome owing to the seriousness of the illness. "[T]he case fatality rate is extremely high and [the] mortality rate [is almost] 40%," writes Hussain.[44]

Still another Category C pathogen—or pathogens in this case—are the bacteria that produce Multidrug Resistant Tuberculosis (MDR-TB). Formidable microorganisms, they are impervious to two medications, isoniazid and rifampin, widely regarded as the most effective drugs to treat tuberculosis.[45] Of course, an untreatable TB epidemic would be a social, political, and medical nightmare, this dread illness that can be spread through a cough or a sneeze.

Additional emergent pathogens in Category C include hantaviruses (bunyaviruses), which may lead to a grave respiratory condition known as Hantavirus Pulmonary Syndrome; the H1N1 virus, which causes a severe form of influenza; the insect-borne Chikungunya virus, which produces Chikungunya Fever in humans; and the Nipah Virus (NiV), a Henipavirus that causes Nipah Virus Infection, a daunting illness that can kill both animals and humans through such complications as encephalitis and severe respiratory conditions. At present, many other pathogenic agents are contained in Category C, a classification that is continually being updated to reflect the arrival of threatening biological agents that could prove appealing to organizations that wish to engage in bioterrorism.

The Weaponization of Pathogens and Toxins

As one would expect, a prospective bioterror attack that would inflict any of the illnesses described in the foregoing section is a reason for vigilance, but contrary to the sensationalized scenarios that the popular media so often depict, devising and deploying a bioweapon is no simple matter. Most terrorist groups are clearly not in a position to pull off such a feat. As we have noted, the types of agents most apt to be converted into biological weapons are pathogens—living organisms that reproduce within the victim—or their derivatives, toxins, which are not alive and do not reproduce but may nevertheless sicken or kill the person. And neither pathogens nor toxins are easily transformed into weapons of mass destruction.

Choice of Pathogen. Of these two broad groupings of agents, pathogens and toxins, perpetrators would most likely select pathogens, since they tend to be more destructive to a population. "Gram for gram," write Nadine Gurr and Benjamin Cole, "[toxins] are less deadly than certain living pathogens because they do not reproduce themselves within the victim, and since they are not contagious they cannot spread beyond the victims that are immediately exposed."[46]

Within the category of pathogens, moreover, are four subcategories of infectious entities, two of which, bacteria and viruses, are the most apt to be used in bioterror attacks. And here again, important differences are readily apparent. "Although it takes hundreds or thousands of bacteria to infect a person, it may take as few as one to ten viral organisms to infect the same person," says Albert Mauroni.[47] Then, too, vaccines have been developed to prevent many bacterial infections, while antibiotics are widely available to treat those that nevertheless manage to occur. By comparison, there are no vaccines to prevent most viral infections and only a few medications to treat them, with supportive care being the standard intervention until the illness runs its course or the victim succumbs. Still, bacteria carry a distinct advantage for would-be bioterrorists. "[B]acteria are often more sturdy than viruses," says Mauroni, "which die off quickly in the natural environment if not incubating in a host."[48] And it is this last feature, bacteria's greater resilience in the natural environment, that contributes to their value as weapons.

Weaponization. After having selected a pathogen or toxin, the perpetrators must next come up with the proficiency to convert it into a weapon. In the event that bacterial entities are chosen, such as powdered anthrax spores, they must be isolated, cultivated, and concentrated, then dried, milled, and aerosolized, a complex undertaking far beyond the capabilities of most terrorist groups. The organization would therefore need to hire or otherwise secure the services of those who possess such highly specialized skills and who have access to the necessary equipment.

Lastly, a decision must be made, when weaponizing a biological agent, about its means of delivery. Depending on the entity and the circumstances of the envisioned attack, the options may be limited. Some agents can only be spread by direct contact with other people or other life forms, such as insects; others require the ingestion of food or water; and still others must be inhaled. What is *not* a consideration is the use of an incendiary device, since the explosion would kill the pathogen. In the succeeding pages, each of these five methods of delivery will be explored, beginning with deliberate human contact with an intended victim pool.

Transmission: Person-to-Person

Perhaps the simplest method of triggering an epidemic is by setting loose the bioterror equivalent of suicide bombers, or what Rohit Puskoor and Geoffrey Zubay refer to as "suicide carriers."[49] These are individuals who permit a terrorist organization to infect them with a pathogen, then surreptitiously introduce the microorganism into the target population.

A smallpox epidemic could be initiated in this manner, according to Puskoor and Zubay, since the disease is readily spread by sneezing or coughing in the vicinity of other people. "Although it seems likely that infected carriers would be too ill and the rash too noticeable for terrorists to be able to infect a large number of people without detection," they write, "the disease is mild enough in its early stages that the rash could be disguised and an infected carrier could be given drugs to moderate symptoms."[50] Furthermore, it would not require an army of suicide carriers to conduct an effective operation. "A few infected individuals in densely packed cities, distant from one another, could infect enough people to cause major epidemics."[51] As to the calculated positioning of smallpox carriers in various metropolises, the strategy would be to overburden the public health system. Fortunately, the fact that the world's only remaining vials of smallpox, being stored in high-security repositories, are inaccessible to terrorist organizations means it is highly unlikely that this particular scenario will ever come to pass, although an outbreak of SARS or similar disease is a realistic possibility.

As Columbia University's Joseph Ward and Maria Garrido caution, suicide carriers hoping to initiate an epidemic of Severe Acute Respiratory Syndrome could infect themselves with the virus that causes it, "then travel on multiple airplanes or otherwise put [themselves] into contact with many people."[52] And while the ensuing illnesses would probably not prove fatal to the preponderance of the victims, their massive number would still cause social instability, including economic strain brought about by temporary reductions in the workforce. Moreover, because most SARS cases are not fatal, the suicide carriers would themselves have a reasonable chance of survival. "[T]hey might not die, and they might not even be suspected of acting as terrorists," write Ward and Garrido."[53] And yet, the possibility of survival notwithstanding, the consequences for those who knowingly transport infectious diseases are grim, so grim as to discourage potential carriers from participating in such a mission. Bioterrorists planning an attack of this type might therefore decide to substitute "vectors," or animals, for human carriers.

Transmission: Vector-Borne

A vector, or "carrier," is an organism that is capable of transmitting an infectious disease from an animal to a human or between humans.[54] Most often, the vector is a mosquito that feasts on an infected animal and, in the process, contracts a pathogen, which it then transmits to the entities it feeds upon, human or animal. Other insects that spread disease in this way include, but are not limited to, ticks, fleas, and sandflies. It is, moreover, a mode of transmission that public health officials take very seriously. "Vector-borne diseases account for more than 17% of all infectious diseases," reports the World Health Organization, "causing more than 1 million deaths annually."[55]

Among such infections that affect humans are Lyme Disease, tularemia, encephalitis, Q fever, and a dreadful illness known as Crimean-Congo Hemorrhagic Fever, all of which are transmitted by ticks. Plague, typhus, and Rocky Mountain spotted fever are also vector-related illnesses, being transmitted by fleas. And mosquitoes spread numerous diseases, among them yellow fever, malaria, Zika Virus Disease (ZVD), Chikungunya, Dengue fever, and encephalitis. This last condition, encephalitis, will serve as an example of the way in which bioterrorists could exploit this infective process.

To devise a biological weapon that would, for instance, cause West Nile encephalitis (WNE), the vector-borne method might involve enclosing a large number of mosquitoes in a room with an animal infected with the virus. By feeding on it, the mosquitoes would contract the pathogen, with the next step being to capture and contain the insects. "To collect the newly diseased mosquitoes, the temperature of the room [would] be lowered, which [would] induce a mosquito hibernation state, allowing the mosquitoes to be gathered in inconspicuous containers," explains Salwa Touma.[56] Subsequent to this, the containers would be transported to the target region, which might consist of a handful of points in a major metropolitan area, then opened to release the insects. Soon, an outbreak of WNE would unnerve the city.

Although West Nile encephalitis is not contagious, the abrupt appearance of an excessive number of cases would likely trigger a public health emergency, one that might go initially unrecognized as a terrorist offensive. "If this form of weaponization were carried out in warmer months," adds Touma, "suspicion would be decreased; hospitals would be contaminated and the number of cases would be uncontrollable by the time terrorism could be implicated."[57]

To make the virus in this scenario even more dangerous, the pathogen could be genetically modified it to enhance its lethality, assuming the biotechnologists working with the terrorist organization possessed the know-how and state-of-the-art equipment to do so.

Transmission: Foodborne

Another means by which perpetrators may sicken or kill unsuspecting citizens involves poisoning the food supply, a method that has been successfully employed in several biocrimes and a small number of bioterror operations. Pathogens, such as the *Salmonella enterica* bacterium, and toxins, like ricin and *Clostridium botulinum*, are strong candidates for food contamination, since they are not necessarily difficult to obtain and they produce dramatic symptoms when ingested. All the same, the majority of pathogenic microorganisms are only effective as bioweapons, or at least at their most damaging, when they are inhaled, injected, absorbed, or taken into the body through other means. As Kira Morser and her colleagues point out, however, it might be possible to genetically engineer one or more of the latter pathogens to enable them to function as food contaminants as well.[58]

While many experts contend that it is comparatively easy to poison a population by tainting the food supply—they point to *Salmonella enterica* as being easy to isolate and cultivate—others insist that foodborne bio-attacks are actually quite difficult to accomplish and seldom fatal.[59] This is especially the case for those that make use of bacteria, since standard food preparation measures usually neutralize them. "Cooking, boiling, pasteurization, and other routine safety precautions are generally sufficient to kill pathogenic bacteria," says Jonathan Tucker.[60] But as a 1984 bioterror offensive in Oregon revealed, tainting salad dressings, coffee creamers, fruit, and vegetables with a slurry that contains *S. enterica* is sufficient to poison scores of unwary diners.

Of course, a foodborne bioterror operation would not necessarily need to kill masses of people to achieve its aims, namely attracting news coverage, alarming the population, or otherwise disrupting society. "For rogue groups wishing to spread panic," says Morser, "causing people to doubt the safety of anything they might eat could be a very powerful psychological tool."[61]

Transmission: Waterborne

The same holds true when people have reason to suspect that their drinking water may be contaminated. The fact is, there are numerous pathogens and toxins that are effective as bioweapons when introduced into the water supply, with some of them, such as the bacteria that cause cholera and shigellosis, functioning remarkably well in this medium. Not only that, biological agents that are usually disseminated in other ways can sometimes be altered to serve as waterborne bioweapons as well.

To use a pathogen or toxin to this end, four criteria must be met, according to Donald Hickman of the Air War College at Maxwell Air Force Base.[62] Generally speaking, the perpetrator must be able to produce and distribute the agent in a sizable enough quantity to ensure it will be destructive to the target population. It must also be capable of retaining its structure and virulence once it is deposited in a watery milieu. Moreover, the agent, if it is a pathogen, must remain infectious in drinking water, since this will be the final medium before human consumption. And lastly, it must be able to survive the chlorination and filtration that occurs at water processing facilities.

As it happens, the latter—chlorination and filtration—comprise one of the chief obstacles to implementing a successful water-based bioterror operation, the other being the moderating effects of dilution. Together, these actions will thwart the vast majority of water-based attacks.

Looking more closely at the role of dilution in particular, its mitigating effects can be seen in those cases in which the perpetrating organization hopes to harm a population by releasing pathogens or toxins in a river, lake, or other large body of water. In such instances, the immense amount of water will eclipse the comparatively tiny amount of pathogenic material, neutralizing it or at least markedly reducing its harmfulness. Ensuring the success of a bio-attack of this sort, then, would likely require a considerable quantity of pathogens or toxins, far more than a terrorist group might be able to obtain without being detected. This is why most such outfits would probably turn to another mode of attack. "Targeting of large bodies of water such as water supply reservoirs would be impractical," write Dickinson Burrow and Sara Renner.[63]

As an aside, it is worth noting that the diluting effects of air are even greater than those of water, since open air, unlike a lake or reservoir, has no physical boundaries. Thus, an airborne attack, depending on the type of agent used, might well require a vaster amount of pathogenic material. Then, too, water, compared to air, carries additional benefits as a medium for a biological assault. "[I]n many cases," writes Hickman, "the materials are more stable (protected from ultraviolet and temperature extremes, although exposed to chlorine.)"[64] Even so, this last factor, chlorination, should not be underestimated.

As it stands, the list of pathogens that are capable of being weaponized and functioning as threats in water is a fairly long one, and includes the bacteria that cause plague, tularemia, salmonella, shigellosis, anthrax, and Q fever, among others. However, the chlorine that is normally present in a large, treated water supply will inactivate many, if not most, of these agents, with the notable exception of anthrax spores. A study by Jon Calomiris at the Air Force Research Laboratory in Edgewood, Maryland, has demonstrated the resilience of such spores when exposed to the customary quantities of chlorine used in many water processing plants. "The data seem to suggest that anthrax spores can tolerate water treatment, can attach to pipes or biofilms within the pipes, and could pass through pipe systems to reach the consumer tap," Calomiris told an audience at the 2006 meeting of the American Society for Microbiology.[65] Not only do the spores resist chlorine at its standard level of use, however, they also remain stable in water for up to two years.[66] For such reasons, larger concentrations of chlorine would become necessary in the face of a suspected anthrax attack, or, alternatively, the use of substitute disinfectants for protracted periods of time.[67] Naturally, it would be necessary to shut down the water supply until it was deemed safe again.

As for toxins, several can serve as contaminants in water, although, again, chlorine inactivates many of them, even botulinum neurotoxin. But one that is not neutralized is ricin. Impervious to chemical disinfection when the customary levels of chlorine are used, it could be deployed successfully in a bioterror offensive.[68] In an attack of this type, either larger quantities of chlorine would be necessary to deactivate the ricin or the contaminated water would need to be subjected to the process of reverse osmosis.

Taking into account the neutralizing effects of filtration and chlorination, it would be imperative for a terrorist organization hoping to pull off a water-based offensive to devise a means of ensuring that its pathogen or toxin avoided both of these processes. One way the group could do this is by temporarily disabling the water-processing plant's operations so that the agent would not be exposed to either procedure. Another would be to introduce the agent into water that has already been treated; that is, contaminate it at post-processing points located nearer to the target population. "[T]hese might include finished water storage facilities, vulnerable points in the distribution system, or even bottled water," write Burrows and Renner.[69]

Regarding the bio-attack's presentation, because a water-based operation is, by its nature, insidious—its arrival is not heralded by a sensational event, such as a bombing—it could impact the population long before anyone realized its occurrence was intentional. "The first evidence of attack is likely to be a flood of sick or dying at the emergency room," writes Hickman. "By the time water is recognized as the source, identification and quantification of the agent could take days if not weeks."[70] Moreover, public health and counterterrorism agencies could face further challenges if the attack were to be executed by a sophisticated organization having access to a variety of microorganisms and toxins coupled with the ability to customize them. "[T]he adversary could tailor the effect based on his objective," says Hickman, "using chemicals or fast acting pathogens for a quick kill, or slower incubating pathogens for delayed effects."[71] The advantage of fast-acting agents is that they can accomplish their mission—harming or killing the victims—before the authorities are able to detect and eliminate them. The advantage of slower-acting agents, on the other hand, is their ability to enter a much larger portion of the population before the attack is discovered and contained. Said differently, a lengthy delay between contracting an infection and symptom formation gives the pathogen more time to reach a greater number of potential victims.

Transmission: Airborne

Arguably the swiftest way for a pathogenic agent to sweep through a population and affect the largest number of people is via the airborne route, with some experts maintaining that this may be the sole means by which a pathogen or toxin could function as a true weapon of mass destruction given the current state of our technology. "The only potential way to inflict mass casualties with a BW agent is by disseminating it as a respirable aerosol," writes Jonathan Tucker, "an invisible cloud of infectious droplets or particles so tiny that they remain suspended in the air for long periods and can be inhaled by large numbers of people."[72] Although the biodefense community continuously monitors developments in person-to-person, waterborne, food-borne, and vector-borne routes of disease transmission, its top concern centers on an airborne attack.

Airborne pathogens or toxins are potentially capable of reaching a vast, heavily populated region if properly deployed, with aerosolized agents tending to be extremely lethal to the victims. The latter is due partly to the microbes' compactness after weaponization. "The particles of bioweapons are very small (approximately 1–5 microns in diameter), and because they are light and fluffy they do not fall to earth very quickly; given the right weather conditions a bioweapon will drift for up to a hundred miles," write Gurr and Cole.[73] Once the particles are inhaled, moreover, another feature comes into play. "Their tiny size means that they are sucked deep into the lungs, where they stick to the membranes and then enter the bloodstream where they begin to replicate."[74] This is why a pathogen, when inhaled, can incapacitate a victim so rapidly, as opposed to being swallowed or introduced through a mosquito bite. That said, aerosolization can be an extremely intricate process, one that can sometimes be accomplished only by professionals working in highly specialized laboratories. And there is a second challenge inherent in this method of transmission: airborne pathogens and toxins, after having been successfully weaponized and released into the atmosphere, must contend with the effects of the physical environment.

The fact is, the preponderance of pathogenic agents are degraded by exposure to oxygen, sunlight, heat, and/or humidity, as well as being neutralized by shock or dehydration. The Ebola virus, for instance, is rapidly deactivated when it makes contact with air, while the bacteria that cause plague and tularemia are incapacitated by the ultraviolet radiation of the sun's rays. Similarly, the pathogen that produces botulism is degraded by warm temperatures and humidity. And then there is the weather, with a rainy day washing away any bioweapon that a terrorist group might release into the atmosphere. Not that an arid day is without its downside. "On a summer day," says Mauroni, "the winds would probably carry a released agent straight up and disperse it without causing any casualties."[75] For such reasons, biodefense experts believe a night-time release of an aerosolized agent would meet with the most success, a period of several hours during which heat, moisture, and ultraviolet radiation would be at their lowest levels.[76] As an alternative, an early-morning release on an overcast day would also be effective.[77] Then again, a perpetrator could deploy an airborne agent in a confined space, such as an office building or subway, where it would avoid exposure to wind, rain, and other elements, while also having immediate access to a concentrated victim pool. Such scenarios, it should be pointed out, have been openly discussed in the biodefense community for several years, as well as appearing in books and articles available to the public.

Turning to the various biological agents that are capable of being aerosolized, bioterror experts express an abundance of concern about the anthrax bacterium. Certainly their worry is not misplaced. Besides North America, naturally-occurring anthrax is available in Australia, Africa, Asia, and southern Europe, frequently in the soil. In addition, it is better able to withstand sunlight and aridity than many other airborne bacteria, as well as being more adaptable to extreme temperatures, both low and high. All in all, it is a remarkably hardy microorganism. "In ambient conditions," writes Anuj Mehta, "the anthrax spore can survive for decades, if not longer."[78] And still another plus for bioterrorists is that the agent, unlike other microorganisms, does not proclaim its presence. "[A]nthrax is extremely attractive as a bioweapon because the aerosolized form has no odor, is essentially colorless (depending on the method of aerosolization), and is virtually undetectable," Mehta adds."[79]

This brings us to the "Amerithrax" offensive, a case in which anthrax-laced letters were dispatched to media and political figures in the wake of the September 11th attacks on the World Trade Center and Pentagon. In this malevolent episode, anthrax was converted into a powdered bioweapon, the pathogen being so finely milled that its particles literally floated in the air. And this near-weightlessness contributed to the weapon's lethality. When suspended in such a manner, spores can be carried long distances by air currents and, of course, inhaled, with their tiny size permitting them to lodge intractably in the lungs. In Chapter Eight, the Amerithrax episode, the first anthrax attack in the nation's history, is recounted in detail, including a look at the manner in which the pathogen was converted into such a remarkable weapon.

Even more fearsome than aerosolized anthrax is the engineering of a hybrid entity—a "superbug"—that could likewise be disseminated through the air. It is already suspected that some nations have attempted to devise microorganisms of this sort, with perhaps the scariest such concoction being a supervirus known as "Ebolapox." According to a source who played a role in the former Soviet Union's biowarfare program, there is reason to believe the USSR may have created such an entity by splicing together segments of the Ebola and smallpox genomes, the result of which would be a hybrid that is more robust and deadlier than either the Ebola virus or the variola (smallpox) virus alone.[80] "A weapon composed of Ebolapox," write Rohit Puskoor and Geoffrey Zubay, "would possess the violent hemorrhaging and high fatality rate characteristic of the Ebola virus and the contagiousness of the smallpox virus."[81] Symptomatically, its features would include hemorrhaging under the skin, which would cause the skin to blacken as part of a condition known as pruritic smallpox or "blackpox." Not surprisingly, Ebolapox would probably kill up to a hundred percent of those who contracted it.[82]

Certainly bioterror organizations, by manipulating the genetic codes of other airborne pathogens or toxins, could enhance their lethality as well. For instance, pathogens' resistance to environmental conditions, such as radiation and desiccation, could be augmented, thereby increasing their survival time when released into the atmosphere. For bacterial and viral entities in particular, their resistance to medical interventions—vaccines, antibiotics, and antiviral medications—could be enhanced, rendering them even more resilient. To be sure, advances in genetic engineering, while profoundly beneficial to humankind, may well permit bioterrorists to transform existent airborne pathogens and toxins into even more pernicious tools of aggression. And this applies equally to those biological agents that spread from person to person or through insect bites, the water supply, food products, and other means.

In the succeeding chapters, the calculated exploitation of the bacteria and viruses that cause typhoid fever, AIDS, hepatitis C, shigellosis, anthrax, and salmonella poisoning will be illustrated through real-life cases in which they were deployed against targeted individuals or populations. Included, too, will be an episode in which ricin, one of the deadliest toxins in existence, was used as a murder weapon, and another in which the nerve gas sarin, a chemical agent and weapon of mass destruction, was deployed after perpetrators failed to execute an assault using infectious microorganisms. Five of the cases are classified as biocrimes while the remaining two constituted acts of bioterrorism. Collectively, they demonstrate the diverse motives for, and methods of, attack that have been explored in the preceding chapters, together with the pathogens and toxins that perpetrators most often select for their reprehensible campaigns to bring harm to the unsuspecting.

◆ 5 ◆

Bad Medicine

Biocrime in the Healthcare Professions

A biocrime can be committed by most anyone provided that the person has access to a biological agent such as a bacterium or virus, possesses the technical know-how to perform the deed, and has the opportunity to carry it out. The biocriminals whose acts are the focus of the present chapter not only fulfill these criteria rather handily, but are also believed to comprise the largest category of perpetrators.

The fact is, biocrimes in the United States are committed to a disproportionate extent by those who work in medical settings, precisely the types of men and women most of us would never expect to intentionally inflict harm on others. With a modicum of reflection, however, it becomes apparent why healthcare workers would, in fact, be among the most frequent offenders. From hospitals to dental clinics, medical facilities are home to an array of pathogens, some of them potentially lethal, with those who work in such settings being well-versed in the illnesses these sorts of entities produce.

Then, too, a healthcare milieu offers a ready-made victim pool, since those with whom medical professionals interact on a routine basis—patients—are, by definition, ill or at least registered to receive medical treatment. As a 2001 editorial in the *British Medical Journal* suggests about biocriminals in the medical sphere, it is plausible that "all walks of life have people with the potential to murder ... (but the) key difference may be opportunity."[1]

It is certainly easy to spot the rich possibilities that a medical environment offers the would-be biocriminal. In such a setting, a prospective target, especially if seriously ill and hospitalized, may be bedridden, weak, sedated, and isolated from others; vulnerable circumstances by any measure. In addition, the potential victim's medical team, family, and friends, since they already perceive the person as being in the sick role, may not be suspicious of a change or worsening of his or her symptoms. Surely it is a fact that even in the most dramatic cases, meaning those in which a biocrime leads to a debilitating malady or death, the questions that arise invariably focus on the reason that the patient's original ailment took such a devastating turn. Accordingly, the standard response, particularly when the emergent features are inconsistent with those of the preexisting ailment, is to perform an expanded workup; a conventional search for a natural cause in an effort to reconcile the disparate symptoms.

Still another reason that healthcare workers, compared to those in other professions, may be inclined to execute biocrimes centers on the profound trust that is customarily placed in them and in medical institutions in general, a trust demonstrated by patients' unthinking submission to invasive measures. "Only in a healthcare setting will normal people allow a stranger to stick them with a needle and administer potentially injurious substances," says Kenneth Iverson, a bioethicist and physician who practices emergency medicine in Tucson, Arizona.[2] Surely it is true that patients routinely entrust their lives to the staffs of medical facilities, where they encounter steady streams of caregivers about whom they may know nothing other than the names printed on the workers' badges. For the individual wishing to use pathogenic microbes to effect a crime, then, a medical setting offers a remarkable assortment of tools coupled with myriad opportunities and the blind trust of the potential victims.

As to the occupations of the perpetrators, research has shown that nurses make up fifty percent of the offenders, with the crimes, in these studies, being defined as those that employ either biological or chemical agents. A smaller share of offenses, roughly twenty-five percent, are carried out by physicians.[3] It should be noted, though, that the latter number may be misleading; that the figure may actually be higher but that doctors are simply more effective at ensuring their deeds go undetected as well as being better insulated within the medical hierarchy.[4] In terms of the remaining twenty-five percent, it is comprised of dentists, opticians, nurses' aides, and orderlies, among others.[5]

Regarding the victims, patients are highly represented, of course, although fellow medical professionals have also been targeted, as have romantic partners. Family members have likewise found themselves in the crosshairs, most often spouses. And in a handful of instances, perpetrators have targeted a diversity of individuals, as was the case in Chiba, Japan, in the mid–1960s.

Biocrime Files

The Mitsuru Suzuki Case

Doctors, nurses, patients, family members, and even a military officer were the victims of Mitsuru Suzuki, a physician who embarked on a residency in microbiology only to find himself galled by what he described as "the seniority system which prevails in medical circles."[6] Angry because he felt that the higher-ups in his training program at Chiba University Hospital in Eastern Japan were discriminating against him—Suzuki was convinced they were treating him unfairly because he had graduated from a medical school other than the one at Chiba University—he was further irritated because his spot in the residency was unpaid and, he suspected, temporary. For this reason, he felt the need to extract revenge. But Suzuki had another pressing need as well: he was conducting bacteriological research and required more participants. So it was that he came up with a means of satisfying both needs, a plan that was both crafty and creative, not to mention criminal. He decided to punish the "enemy"—the medical establishment—by exposing both healthcare workers and patients to pathogenic bacteria, thereby transforming them into valuable research subjects. It was shortly before Christmas in 1964 that he put his devious plot into motion.

Purchasing a sponge cake at a shop near Chiba University Hospital where his residency was based, Suzuki contaminated it with *Shigella dysenteriae*. How he obtained this agent which causes bacillary dysentery has never been determined. Later that day, he presented the cake to four of his colleagues at the hospital, who soon became ill and were admitted for treatment. According to Iverson, hospital officials suspected that the resentful resident was behind the poisoning episode, which came to be known by the Agatha Christie–like nickname, the "sponge cake incident."[7] Even so, they did not take action against him because they didn't want to embarrass Chiba University Hospital. Certainly the ensuing publicity would not have buoyed the institution's image as a place of healing, but by leaving the perpetrator unaware that officials were now suspicious of him, he felt sufficiently confident to continue poisoning those in his surroundings.

The summer of 1966 would prove to be a very busy one for Suzuki, since it was during this season that he decided to inoculate an assortment of foods with *Salmonella typhi*, the bacterium that causes typhoid fever. He obtained the pathogen from one of his patients, as well as gaining illicit access to it from Japan's National Institute of Health where he also trained on occasion. "I wanted to see how a mass outbreak of disease might develop from the planted bacilli," he later said.[8]

To this end, he introduced *S. typhi* into bottles of a soft drink that contained a milk base and to which his coworkers had easy access. Soon, sixteen of them were diagnosed with typhoid fever. In four of the cases, Suzuki went even further, administering a "medicine" he claimed would ease their discomfort. Unbeknownst to these colleagues, he was actually injecting them with *S. dysenteriae*, meaning they would come down not only with the symptoms of typhoid but dysentery as well.

Curious about other avenues of infection, Suzuki, a short time later, introduced *Shigella* into the nasogastric tube of a patient at a clinic affiliated with the Kawasaki Steel Plant. Such a direct route more or less guaranteed the target would be laid low with a severe case of dysentery, and quite rapidly.

Finally, at the end of summer, the treacherous resident discovered a means of infecting his victims that he would thereafter use in most of his crimes. Having poisoned an internist with *S. typhi* on September 4th with a contaminated cake—innocently enough, the internist shared it with two others, who also become ill—Suzuki began injecting bananas with the bacillus. And he found that this method worked particularly well. In fact, it was so effective that, by year's end, he had caused twenty doctors and nurses to develop typhoid fever by means of adulterated bananas, along with two of their relatives and eight of his own distant relatives. Another thirteen patients at Chiba University Hospital also consumed his tainted bananas, as did a nurse at another hospital. In a particularly unfortunate turn of events, the latter shared the fruit with the deputy director of the Mishima Social Insurance Hospital, a doctor by training, who succumbed to typhoid fever shortly thereafter. Yet even as these maladies were piling up, medical authorities did not point the finger at Suzuki. An investigation, when one finally was set into motion, would be the result of an anonymous tip to the Ministry of Health and Welfare, according to Iverson's account of the case.[9]

In the meantime, Suzuki proceeded with his campaign. Throughout early 1966, he adulterated various medications with *S. typhi*, along with a barium solution that was subsequently distributed to a pair of clinics. He also laced tongue depressors with the bacillus, as well as mandarin oranges that he left in the nurses' break rooms. He even infected a plate of clams served to a military officer.

Largely out of control now, Suzuki next infected his brother and sister-in-law, along with several family friends. And as the numbers of illnesses soared, he phoned local hospitals, under another name, and instructed them to be on the lookout for a rise in typhoid cases. He appears to have been tracking the speed and spread of the outbreak he had initiated.

All told, Suzuki's actions took the lives of four people and infected 120 others.[10] Ensuing estimates were higher, however, with as many as a dozen dead and over four hundred infected.[11] Yet when the time came for the doctor to face the music, the legal system was curiously anemic. In the spring of 1966, Suzuki was indicted on thirteen counts of intentional infection primarily in the form of food contamination, but, inexplicably, he was not charged with murder.

At first, he fessed up to the crimes. On having second thoughts, however, or perhaps deferring to legal counsel, he subsequently withdrew his confession and plead innocent to the charges. In due course, a court found him not guilty on all counts. A puzzling verdict, it may have stemmed, at least in part, from a lack of evidence other than that which was circumstantial. But this is not the end of the story.

In 1982, the case was reopened in large measure because the Japanese medical community's outrage over Suzuki's engineered outbreaks had never subsided. His peers did not believe that justice had been served. And this time the outcome was different: the earlier verdict was reversed, the physician was found guilty, and his medical license, revoked. Furthermore, he would spend the next six years behind bars.

The Diane Thompson Case

Legal action in the United States would be swifter and more severe in the case of Diane Thompson, a clinical laboratory technician at the St. Paul Medical Center in Dallas. Like other medical employees having access to pathogens in the workplace, Thompson's job placed her in proximity to frozen strains of *Shigella dysenteriae*, the same microorganism Mitsuru Suzuki had used in his crimes. Unlike the Japanese physician, however, the twenty-seven-year-old American laid her first trap outside the hospital.

Enmeshed in a romantic relationship having more than its share of ups and downs—Thompson once slashed her boyfriend's tires and dumped sugar in his gas tank—the lab tech decided in 1995 to assault him on another front, a gastrointestinal one.[12] Drawing on her expertise, she contaminated a syringe with an undisclosed pathogen, then used it to extract a sample of his blood. She also laced his food with an unnamed microbe, one that produced fever and diarrhea suggestive of *S. dysenteriae* infection. So severe were these symptoms that it was necessary to hospitalize him. Yet even now Thompson had the upper hand. Because she had access to stool samples and lab test results, she was able to swap his fecal sample with that of another patient, falsify his records, and thereby confound his course of his treatment. "Thompson," writes biowarfare expert Raymond Zilinskas, "managed to fabricate his laboratory reports to prevent the correct diagnosis of his illness."[13] At the time, the boyfriend did not know she had orchestrated his malady, but others did know, or so it was claimed. Thompson's defense attorney would later state that the lab tech's supervisors were aware of her scheme to poison her boyfriend yet did nothing to prevent her from carrying it out.[14]

Just as Mitsuru Suzuki, after infecting four colleagues and believing he had gotten away with it, went on to infect hundreds more, so Thompson, after successfully sickening her boyfriend, proceeded to do the same to her colleagues. On October 29, 1996, a Saturday morning, she dispatched an email to several coworkers at the medical center inviting them to enjoy blueberry muffins, doughnuts, and other treats in the break room. She also continued reminding them about the pastries throughout the morning, even escorting three of them to the break room where she watched them eat the tainted treats. And although some of the targets were only slightly acquainted with Thompson, they had no qualms about accepting her seemingly generous offer. No one suspected anything foul was afoot. In all, thirteen people consumed her breads and pastries.[15]

By the following evening, all of these coworkers were suffering from gastroenteritis, with four of them requiring hospitalization. But with circumstances pointing to the lab tech as the likely perpetrator of the crime—not only had she supplied the pastries, she had also used a bacterium rarely found in the United States but that was present in the medical center's pathogen bank—she soon confessed. During the legal proceedings, Thompson appeared both confused and distraught, and claimed she did not know why she had sickened her colleagues. In the end, a court convicted her of aggravated assault and four felony counts of tampering with consumer products. Sentenced to four concurrent twenty-year terms, she is scheduled for release in 2018.

In terms of the aftermath of the laboratory breach, the St. Paul Medical Center, among other measures, tightened its employees' access to the facility's store of pathogens. As to Thompson's method, medical authorities are still not sure how she devised her bio-weapon from the frozen bacterium pilfered from the laboratory, but they do have an idea. It seems the subject became a matter of speculation at her trial, where a rather simple technique was proposed. "[S]everal microbiologists and medical technologists … said it would be easy to thaw and then grow the bacteria in a solution that could be applied to food as a mist," reports the *Associated Press*.[16]

A similar question, that of method, arose in the case of another medical technician in the Midwest in the mid–1990s, Brian Stewart, who would likewise be charged with a crime involving a pathogenic microbe. As in the Diane Thompson affair, this man's method was never proven, yet there was little doubt about how he had done it, at least in the eyes of the court. So convincing was the prosecutor's circumstantial evidence, in fact, that a conviction was handed down after only a few hours of deliberation by the jury.

The Brian Stewart Case

Employed by Barnes Hospital in St. Louis, Stewart was a twenty-six-year-old phlebotomist, a technician who extracts blood for transfusions, donations, and medical tests. At times, his position placed him in contact with blood or blood products that contained HIV, the lentivirus that leads to AIDS, and for Stewart this apparently proved to be a tempting set of circumstances.